CONTENTS

Connected: The Complete History and Future of the Internet — 1
Chapter 1: The Genesis of Connectivity — 2
Chapter 2: The Birth of TCP/IP — 7
Chapter 3: The Modem Revolution — 16
Chapter 4: The Rise of Bulletin Board Systems (BBSs) — 22
Chapter 5: The Dawn of Graphical User Interfaces (GUIs) — 30
Chapter 6: Windows 95: The Game Changer — 38
Chapter 7: The Backbone of the Internet: TCP/IP Stacks — 46
Chapter 8: Early Online Services: Pioneers of the Digital Age — 56
Chapter 9: The Search for Information: Alta Vista and Beyond — 67
Chapter 10: FidoNet: The Global BBS Network — 77
Chapter 11: The World Wide Web: A New Dimension — 87
Chapter 12: The Impact of Windows 95 and Internet Explorer — 98
Chapter 13: The Dawn of High-Speed Internet — 108
Chapter 14: The Social Web Emerges — 117
Chapter 15: The Internet's Role in Globalization — 129
Chapter 16: The Dark Side of the Internet — 140
Chapter 17: The Evolution of Search Engines — 151

Chapter 18: The Mobile Internet Revolution — 162

Chapter 19: The Cloud and Beyond — 174

Chapter 20: The Internet's Future: Challenges and Opportunities — 188

CONNECTED: THE COMPLETE HISTORY AND FUTURE OF THE INTERNET

By
Tony Yustein © 2024
https://thecode.wiki

CHAPTER 1: THE GENESIS OF CONNECTIVITY

Overview

This chapter explores the birth of the internet, tracing its roots to the creation of ARPANET, the groundbreaking project that laid the foundation for modern networked communication. The chapter examines the Cold War-era motivations that drove the development of ARPANET, the creation of packet switching as a revolutionary method for transmitting data, the first successful communication between computers, and the early adopters of this nascent technology.

Introduction to ARPANET and Its Role in the Cold War Era

The origins of the internet are deeply intertwined with the geopolitical tensions of the Cold War, a period marked by the rivalry between the United States and the Soviet Union. In the late 1950s and early 1960s, the U.S. Department of Defense sought to develop a communication system that could withstand a potential nuclear attack. The fear of a Soviet strike on critical infrastructure, including communication networks, prompted the need for a decentralized and resilient system that could continue functioning even if parts of it were destroyed.

The Advanced Research Projects Agency (ARPA), now known as the Defense Advanced Research Projects Agency (DARPA), was tasked with addressing this challenge. ARPA's mandate was to explore innovative and cutting-edge technologies that could enhance the U.S. military's capabilities. One of its most ambitious projects was the development of a new kind of communication network that could link different computer systems across the country.

In 1966, ARPA initiated the ARPANET project under the leadership of Dr. Lawrence Roberts, who envisioned a network that would allow computers to communicate with one another over long distances. The primary objective was to enable researchers at various universities and government institutions to share information and resources efficiently, thereby accelerating the pace of scientific discovery and technological advancement. ARPANET was not only a response to Cold War pressures but also a means of fostering collaboration among the nation's brightest minds.

The Creation of Packet Switching and Its Significance

At the heart of ARPANET's design was the concept of packet switching, a revolutionary method for transmitting data that differed significantly from the traditional circuit-switched networks used in telephone systems. In a circuit-switched network, a dedicated communication path is established between two points for the duration of a conversation. While effective for voice communication, this method was inefficient for data transmission, especially when dealing with large volumes of data or when the communication path was not continuously in use.

Packet switching, proposed independently by Paul Baran of the RAND Corporation and Donald Davies of the National Physical Laboratory in the United Kingdom, offered a more flexible and efficient solution. In a packet-switched network, data is broken down into smaller units called packets. Each packet is transmitted independently across the network and can take different routes to reach its destination. Once all packets arrive, they are reassembled into the original message.

This method had several key advantages:

1. **Efficiency:** Packet switching made better use of available bandwidth by allowing multiple communications to share the same network paths. Since packets could be routed through any available path, the network could adapt to congestion and continue functioning even if some paths were compromised.
2. **Resilience:** The decentralized nature of packet switching meant that the network did not rely on a single point of failure. If part of the network was destroyed, packets could still find alternative routes, ensuring the continuity of communication.
3. **Scalability:** As the network grew, packet switching allowed for the seamless addition of new nodes (computers) without the need for extensive reconfiguration.

The implementation of packet switching was a critical breakthrough that made ARPANET possible. It laid the foundation for the development of the Transmission Control Protocol (TCP) and the Internet Protocol (IP), which would later become the core protocols of the internet.

The First Successful Communication Between Computers

The first successful communication between computers on the ARPANET took place on October 29, 1969. This historic event occurred between the University of California, Los Angeles (UCLA), and the Stanford Research Institute (SRI). The two institutions were among the first nodes connected to ARPANET, along with the University of California, Santa Barbara (UCSB), and the University of Utah.

The initial message was intended to be the word "LOGIN." However, due to a system crash after the first two letters were sent, the first message ever transmitted over ARPANET was simply "LO." Despite this technical hiccup, the significance of the moment was clear: two computers, located hundreds of miles apart, had successfully communicated with each other over a shared network.

This rudimentary exchange marked the beginning of a new era in communication. The ability to transmit data between computers in real-time opened up a world of possibilities for collaboration, research, and eventually, the development of the global internet. The initial success of ARPANET set the stage for further expansion and experimentation, as more institutions joined the network and explored its potential.

The Early Adopters of Networked Communication

The early adopters of ARPANET were primarily academic and research institutions, which recognized the potential of this new technology for advancing their work. These institutions played a crucial role in the development and expansion of the network, contributing both to the technical innovations that made it possible and to the culture of collaboration that it fostered.

- **University of California, Los Angeles (UCLA):** As the first node on ARPANET, UCLA was instrumental in the network's initial deployment. The university's team, led by Professor Leonard Kleinrock, conducted the first successful communication with SRI, demonstrating the viability of the network.
- **Stanford Research Institute (SRI):** SRI was another early node on ARPANET and played a key role in the network's development. SRI's work on network protocols and interfaces helped shape the way computers would communicate over ARPANET and, by extension, the internet.
- **University of California, Santa Barbara (UCSB):** UCSB was an early participant in ARPANET, contributing to the network's development and exploring its potential

- **University of Utah:** The University of Utah was one of the original four nodes on ARPANET, and its involvement in the network helped to expand its reach and capabilities. The university's computer graphics research would later contribute to the development of pioneering technologies in the field.

These institutions, along with others that joined ARPANET in its early years, were the pioneers of networked communication. They laid the groundwork for the internet by experimenting with new ways of sharing information, collaborating across distances, and pushing the boundaries of what was technically possible. Their contributions were not only technical but also cultural, as they helped to create the ethos of openness and collaboration that continues to define the internet today.

Conclusion

The genesis of connectivity through ARPANET was a critical moment in the history of the internet. Driven by the strategic imperatives of the Cold War and propelled by groundbreaking innovations like packet switching, ARPANET demonstrated the feasibility of a decentralized communication network. The early successes and contributions of pioneering institutions set the stage for the rapid expansion of networked communication, leading ultimately to the creation of the global internet. As we explore the subsequent chapters, we will see how these early developments laid the foundation for the digital world we inhabit today.

CHAPTER 2: THE BIRTH OF TCP/IP

Overview

This chapter delves into the pivotal development of the Transmission Control Protocol (TCP) and the Internet Protocol (IP), two foundational technologies that have become the backbone of modern internet communication. We will explore the visionary work of Vint Cerf and Bob Kahn, who invented these protocols, the transition of ARPANET to the TCP/IP protocol suite, the global adoption of TCP/IP as the standard for networking, and the profound impact these protocols have had on the expansion and evolution of the internet.

The Invention of TCP/IP by Vint Cerf and Bob Kahn

The creation of TCP/IP is often hailed as one of the most significant milestones in the history of the internet. It was born out of the necessity to develop a robust, scalable, and reliable method for connecting disparate networks and allowing them to communicate seamlessly.

Background and Motivation: In the early 1970s, ARPANET had demonstrated the feasibility of networked communication, but it was limited to a relatively small number of connected nodes (computers) within a single network. As the idea of networking expanded, so did the need for a protocol that could support communication between different types of networks—such as local area networks (LANs), satellite networks, and radio-based networks—each with its own unique characteristics and requirements.

Vint Cerf and Bob Kahn, two visionary computer scientists, recognized this need. Bob Kahn, who had been working on ARPANET, was particularly concerned with the challenges of inter-network communication. In 1973, he invited Vint Cerf to collaborate on developing a solution. Cerf, who had a deep understanding of networking protocols from his previous work, quickly became an essential partner in this endeavor.

The Development of TCP/IP: Cerf and Kahn proposed a revolutionary approach to networking that involved breaking down data into packets that could be transmitted independently across multiple networks and then reassembled at their destination. This method was based on the concept of packet switching, which had already been implemented in ARPANET, but Cerf and Kahn sought to generalize and expand this approach to work across any type of network.

The result of their collaboration was the Transmission Control Protocol (TCP) and the Internet Protocol (IP), collectively known as TCP/IP. The protocols were designed to be flexible and adaptable, capable of handling the transmission of data across networks with varying characteristics and ensuring that the data arrived intact and in the correct order.

Key Features of TCP/IP:

1. **Layered Architecture:** TCP/IP was designed with a layered architecture that separated different aspects of networking into distinct layers, each with its own responsibilities. The Internet Protocol (IP) handled the routing of packets from the source to the destination, while the Transmission Control Protocol (TCP) ensured that the packets were delivered reliably and in the correct sequence.

2. **End-to-End Principle:** One of the core principles of TCP/IP was the end-to-end principle, which stated that the network should be as simple as possible,

with most of the intelligence and complexity residing at the endpoints (the computers at either end of a communication). This allowed the network itself to be more robust and scalable.

3. **Scalability and Flexibility:** TCP/IP was designed to be scalable, allowing it to support a growing number of networks and devices. Its flexible architecture made it adaptable to a wide range of network technologies, from wired Ethernet to wireless radio networks.

The invention of TCP/IP was a breakthrough that addressed the limitations of earlier networking protocols and laid the groundwork for the future expansion of the internet. Cerf and Kahn's work was formally documented in a series of papers published in the mid-1970s, and the protocols were tested and refined through a series of experiments.

The Transition of ARPANET to the TCP/IP Protocol Suite

The transition of ARPANET from its original Network Control Protocol (NCP) to the TCP/IP protocol suite was a critical step in the evolution of the internet. This transition was not only a technical milestone but also a pivotal moment that demonstrated the viability of TCP/IP as the standard for network communication.

The Limitations of NCP: By the early 1970s, ARPANET had grown significantly, connecting more nodes and becoming an increasingly important tool for research and communication. However, the Network Control Protocol (NCP), which had been used to manage communication between nodes on ARPANET, had several limitations. NCP was designed specifically for ARPANET's architecture and could not easily accommodate the growing diversity of networks that were being developed.

As a result, NCP's inability to support inter-network communication became a significant bottleneck. The need for a more versatile protocol that could handle different types of networks became increasingly apparent.

The ARPANET Transition Plan: In 1981, after years of development and testing, TCP/IP was ready to be deployed on a larger scale. The decision was made to transition ARPANET from NCP to TCP/IP. This transition required significant planning and coordination, as every node on the network had to be upgraded to support the new protocol.

The transition plan involved several key steps:

1. **Development of TCP/IP Implementations:** Implementations of TCP/IP were developed for the various operating systems used on ARPANET. This ensured that all nodes would be compatible with the new protocol.
2. **Testing and Simulation:** Extensive testing was conducted to simulate the transition and identify potential issues. This included testing how TCP/IP would handle different types of network traffic and how it would interact with existing network infrastructure.
3. **Coordinated Rollout:** The transition was scheduled to take place on January 1, 1983, a date that became known as "Flag Day." On this day, all nodes on ARPANET were required to switch from NCP to TCP/IP. This coordinated effort was critical to ensuring a smooth transition without disrupting network communication.

Flag Day: January 1, 1983: On January 1, 1983, ARPANET officially transitioned to the TCP/IP protocol suite. The success of this transition demonstrated the robustness and scalability of TCP/IP, and it marked the beginning of a new era in networking.

The transition also highlighted the importance of open standards and collaboration. The development and adoption of TCP/IP involved contributions from researchers and engineers across multiple institutions and organizations. This collaborative approach helped ensure that TCP/IP would become a universal standard, capable of supporting a wide range of networks and applications.

The Global Adoption of TCP/IP as the Standard Networking Protocol

Following the successful transition of ARPANET to TCP/IP, the protocol suite quickly gained traction as the standard for networking, not only in the United States but around the world. The global adoption of TCP/IP was driven by several factors, including its technical superiority, its openness, and the growing demand for interconnected networks.

Technical Superiority: TCP/IP's layered architecture and end-to-end principle made it an ideal solution for networking. It was flexible enough to support a wide range of applications, from simple file transfers to complex, real-time communication. Additionally, TCP/IP was designed to be robust and scalable, allowing it to handle the growing volume of network traffic as more devices and networks were connected.

Openness and Accessibility: One of the key reasons for TCP/IP's widespread adoption was its openness. Unlike some proprietary networking protocols, TCP/IP was developed as an open standard, with detailed specifications available to anyone who wanted to implement it. This openness encouraged innovation and experimentation, as developers around the world could create their own implementations and applications based on TCP/IP.

The Role of the National Science Foundation (NSF): In the 1980s, the National Science Foundation (NSF) played a crucial role in promoting the adoption of TCP/IP. The NSF funded the creation of the NSFNET, a high-speed backbone network that connected regional and academic networks across the United States. NSFNET used TCP/IP as its networking protocol, which helped establish it as the standard for academic and research institutions.

International Adoption: As the internet expanded beyond the United States, TCP/IP was adopted by networks and institutions around the world. European research networks, such as the European Academic and Research Network (EARN) and the CERN (European Organization for Nuclear Research) network, embraced TCP/IP as the standard for their communication infrastructure.

In the Asia-Pacific region, countries like Japan, Australia, and South Korea also adopted TCP/IP, often through collaborations with American universities and research institutions. By the late 1980s and early 1990s, TCP/IP had become the de facto standard for networking on a global scale.

The Impact of TCP/IP on the Expansion of the Internet

The adoption of TCP/IP had a profound impact on the expansion of the internet. Its flexible and scalable architecture allowed the internet to grow rapidly, connecting an ever-increasing number of networks, devices, and users.

Enabling the Growth of the World Wide Web: The development of the World Wide Web in the early 1990s was made possible by TCP/IP. The web's hypertext-based system relied on the reliable and efficient transmission of data provided by TCP/IP. As the web grew in popularity, the demand for internet connectivity surged, driving further expansion of TCP/IP networks.

Support for Emerging Applications: TCP/IP's versatility allowed it to support a wide range of applications beyond simple data transmission. The development of new protocols and applications, such as the Simple Mail Transfer Protocol (SMTP) for email and the File Transfer Protocol (FTP) for file sharing, further expanded the utility of TCP/IP.

Commercialization and the Birth of the Internet Service Provider (ISP) Industry: The adoption of TCP/IP also paved the way for the commercialization of the internet. As businesses and consumers sought to connect to the internet, the demand for internet service providers (ISPs) grew. ISPs provided the infrastructure and services necessary for individuals and organizations to connect to the global TCP/IP **network, further**

accelerating the expansion of the internet.

The commercialization of the internet in the early 1990s was a key turning point in its history. Companies like Prodigy, America Online (AOL), and CompuServe began offering internet access to the general public, often bundling email, web browsing, and other services into easy-to-use packages. These early ISPs relied on TCP/IP to deliver reliable and efficient connectivity, enabling millions of people to access the internet for the first time.

The Role of Government and International Bodies: Governments and international organizations also played a significant role in promoting the adoption of TCP/IP. In the United States, the federal government supported the development of the internet through funding and policy initiatives. The National Science Foundation's NSFNET, for example, was instrumental in expanding the reach of the internet to academic and research institutions across the country.

Internationally, organizations like the Internet Engineering Task Force (IETF) and the Internet Corporation for Assigned Names and Numbers (ICANN) helped standardize and coordinate the development of the internet, ensuring that TCP/IP remained the foundational protocol for global communication. These organizations facilitated the development of new protocols, standards, and technologies that built on TCP/IP, further enhancing its capabilities and reach.

The Expansion of the Global Internet: As TCP/IP became the global standard, the internet began to expand beyond its original academic and research roots. Businesses, governments, and individuals around the world started to recognize the potential of the internet as a tool for communication, commerce, and innovation. The adoption of TCP/IP by these diverse groups contributed to the rapid growth of the internet in the 1990s and beyond.

One of the most significant impacts of TCP/IP was its role in enabling the development of the World Wide Web. The web, invented by Tim Berners-Lee at CERN in 1989, quickly became the dominant application on the internet. TCP/IP provided the underlying infrastructure that allowed web browsers to communicate with web servers, enabling the seamless exchange of information across the globe.

The Emergence of New Applications and Services: The flexibility of TCP/IP also allowed for the development of new applications and services that took advantage of the internet's global reach. Email, for example, became one of the first "killer apps" of the internet, revolutionizing the way people communicated across distances. Other applications, such as instant messaging, Voice over IP (VoIP), and online gaming, also emerged, each relying on the robust capabilities of TCP/IP.

As more and more applications were developed, the demand for internet access continued to grow. This, in turn, drove the expansion of internet infrastructure, including the development of high-speed broadband networks, wireless technologies, and data centers. The internet's growth was exponential, with the number of connected devices and users doubling every few years.

The Internet as a Global Platform: By the late 1990s and early 2000s, the internet had become a truly global platform. TCP/IP had enabled the creation of a network of networks, connecting millions of computers and billions of users around the world. The internet was no longer just a tool for academic research or military communication; it had become an essential part of daily life for people in all corners of the globe.

The widespread adoption of TCP/IP also had profound economic and social implications. It enabled the rise of e-commerce, allowing businesses to reach customers in new markets and providing consumers with unprecedented access to goods and services. It also facilitated the spread of information and ideas, contributing to the growth of global knowledge economies and fostering cross-cultural communication.

The Continuing Evolution of TCP/IP: Despite its success, TCP/IP has continued to evolve over the years. New versions of the protocols, such as IPv6, have been developed to address the growing demand for internet addresses and to improve the security and performance of the network. The development of new protocols and standards, such as HTTPS for secure web browsing and TLS for encrypted communication, have also built on the foundation of TCP/IP.

Today, TCP/IP remains the backbone of the internet, supporting a vast array of applications and services that have transformed the way we live, work, and interact. Its invention by Vint Cerf and Bob Kahn, and its subsequent adoption as the global standard for networking, is one of the most important technological achievements of the 20th century. The impact of TCP/IP on the expansion of the internet cannot be overstated; it has enabled the creation of a truly global communication network that continues to shape our world in profound ways.

CHAPTER 3: THE MODEM REVOLUTION

Overview

This chapter provides an in-depth look at the evolution of modems, the devices that played a crucial role in bringing the internet into homes and businesses through telephone lines. We will explore the invention and development of modems, the transition from slow early models to the faster 56k modems, the significant role modems played in the spread of dial-up internet access, and personal stories from early modem users who experienced the dawn of online connectivity.

The Invention and Development of Modems

The Birth of Modems: The term "modem" is a portmanteau of "modulator-demodulator," a device that converts digital data from computers into analog signals that can be transmitted over traditional telephone lines and vice versa. The development of the modem was driven by the need to transmit digital data over the vast and established infrastructure of analog telephone networks.

The origins of the modem can be traced back to the late 1940s and early 1950s, when the U.S. military developed the first modems to connect radar stations. These early modems were large, expensive, and specialized devices that could transmit data at speeds of up to 300 bits per second (bps). They were used primarily for military and government applications, where secure and reliable communication was critical.

Commercialization of Modems: The commercialization of modems began in the 1960s, as businesses and research institutions started to recognize the potential of computer networking. The Bell 103 modem, introduced by AT&T in 1962, was one of the first commercially available modems. It operated at a speed of 300 bps and used frequency-shift keying (FSK) to modulate the data. The Bell 103 modem became the standard for early computer communication, enabling data transmission between computers over standard telephone lines.

As computers became more common in business and academic environments, the demand for modems grew. In the 1970s, a number of companies, including Hayes, Novation, and U.S. Robotics, began producing modems for the emerging personal computer market. These modems were smaller, more affordable, and easier to use than their predecessors, making them accessible to a wider audience.

The Hayes Command Set: A major milestone in the development of modems was the introduction of the Hayes command set, developed by Dale Heatherington and Dennis Hayes in 1981. The Hayes Smartmodem was the first modem to use this command set, which allowed users to control the modem through simple text commands. The Hayes command set became a de facto standard for modems, enabling compatibility across different devices and software. This standardization helped drive the widespread adoption of modems and made it easier for users to connect to bulletin board systems (BBSs) and other online services.

The Transition from Slow Early Modems to the 56k Modem

The Evolution of Modem Speeds: In the early days of computer networking, modem speeds were extremely slow by today's standards. The first commercially available modems operated at 300 bps, which was sufficient for transmitting text-based data but inadequate for more complex applications. As the demand for faster data transmission grew, modem technology evolved to support higher speeds.

Throughout the 1980s and early 1990s, modem manufacturers introduced a series of innovations that significantly increased modem speeds. The introduction of error correction and data compression techniques allowed modems to transmit data more efficiently, effectively doubling or tripling their throughput. Modems capable of operating at 1200 bps, 2400 bps, 4800 bps, and 9600 bps became available, with each new generation offering faster and more reliable communication.

The Breakthrough of the 56k Modem: The pinnacle of dial-up modem technology came in the mid-1990s with the introduction of the 56k modem. Unlike its predecessors, which were limited by the analog nature of telephone lines, the 56k modem took advantage of digital connections between telephone company central offices and internet service providers (ISPs). This allowed the modem to achieve download speeds of up to 56,000 bps, nearly double the speed of previous 28.8k and 33.6k modems.

The development of the 56k modem was driven by two competing standards: the K56flex standard, developed by Rockwell and Lucent Technologies, and the V.90 standard, which was eventually adopted as the industry-wide standard by the International Telecommunication Union (ITU) in 1998. The introduction of the 56k modem revolutionized dial-up internet access, enabling users to download web pages, images, and files much more quickly than before.

While 56k modems were the fastest dial-up modems ever developed, they still had limitations. The maximum achievable speed was often reduced by the quality of the telephone line, and the upload speeds were typically limited to 33.6 kbps. Nevertheless, the 56k modem represented the peak of dial-up technology and became the standard for internet access until the advent of broadband connections.

The Role of Modems in the Spread of Dial-Up Internet Access

The Growth of Dial-Up Internet: The widespread adoption of modems played a crucial role in the expansion of the internet in the 1980s and 1990s. Before the advent of broadband connections, dial-up internet was the primary means by which individuals and businesses connected to the internet. Modems allowed users to establish a temporary connection to an ISP using a standard telephone line, enabling them to access email, browse the web, and participate in online communities.

As the internet grew in popularity, the demand for modems soared. The mid-1990s saw a boom in the modem market, with millions of households purchasing modems to connect to the internet. ISPs like America Online (AOL), CompuServe, and Prodigy capitalized on this trend by offering easy-to-use software packages that included a modem, making it simple for new users to get online.

The Experience of Dial-Up Internet: Connecting to the internet via dial-up modem was a distinct experience that many early internet users remember well. To establish a connection, users would dial a phone number provided by their ISP, and the modem would emit a series of beeps and hisses as it negotiated a connection with the ISP's server. This process, known as "handshaking," could take several seconds to complete. Once connected, users were charged for the time they spent online, which often led to hurried browsing sessions and a keen awareness of the passage of time.

The limitations of dial-up connections, particularly their slow speeds and the fact that using the internet tied up the household phone line, meant that internet use was often a carefully planned activity. Despite these limitations, dial-up modems were the gateway to the internet for millions of people, enabling them to explore the early web, send and receive emails, and participate in online communities.

Personal Stories from Early Modem Users and Their Experiences

The Thrill of the Early Internet: For many early internet users, the modem represented a gateway to a new and exciting world. The ability to connect to distant computers and communicate with people from around the globe was a novel and thrilling experience. Early adopters often describe the sense of discovery and exploration that accompanied their first forays into the online world.

One common memory among early users is the first time they successfully connected to a BBS or an online service like AOL. The excitement of seeing messages from other users, participating in online forums, or downloading software was palpable. For many, this experience was a turning point that sparked a lifelong interest in technology and the internet.

Challenges and Frustrations: While the modem opened up new possibilities, it also came with its share of challenges and frustrations. Slow connection speeds, frequent disconnections, and busy signals were common complaints among dial-up users. Additionally, the cost of staying online for extended periods could be prohibitive, leading to careful management of online time.

Despite these challenges, early modem users were often resourceful and determined. They learned to navigate the quirks of their modems, experiment with different settings to improve connection quality, and share tips and tricks with others in online communities.

The Impact of Modems on Personal and Professional Lives: For many users, the modem had a profound impact on both their personal and professional lives. It enabled them to work remotely, collaborate with colleagues in different locations, and access a wealth of information that was previously unavailable. For some, the modem even became a tool for building new careers in the burgeoning field of information technology.

Personal stories from this era often highlight the sense of empowerment that came with being able to connect to the world from the comfort of one's own home. The modem democratized access to information and communication, paving the way for the global connectivity we take for granted today.

Conclusion

The modem revolution was a critical chapter in the history of the internet, enabling millions of people to connect to the online world through their existing telephone lines. From the invention of the first modems to the development of the 56k modem, these devices played a crucial role in making the internet accessible to the masses. Despite the limitations of dial-up connections, modems provided a gateway to a new world of information, communication, and community. The personal stories of early modem users reflect the excitement, challenges, and transformative impact of this technology on their lives. As we move forward in this book, we will explore how these early developments laid the groundwork for the broadband revolution and the next phase of internet connectivity.

CHAPTER 4: THE RISE OF BULLETIN BOARD SYSTEMS (BBSS)

Overview

This chapter explores the development and growth of Bulletin Board Systems (BBSs), one of the earliest forms of online communities. BBSs played a crucial role in shaping the way people communicated digitally, laying the groundwork for the social networks and forums we use today. We will examine the creation and evolution of BBSs, delve into the significance of prominent networks like FidoNet, explain how BBSs functioned and what they offered to users, and analyze the cultural impact of BBS communities.

The Creation and Growth of BBSs

The Birth of BBSs: The concept of the Bulletin Board System was born out of a desire to create a digital space where people could communicate, share information, and connect with one another. The first BBS, known as "CBBS" (Computerized Bulletin Board System), was created in 1978 by Ward Christensen and Randy Suess in Chicago. The idea came to Christensen during a snowstorm, when he realized the need for a system that would allow members of a local computer club to exchange messages and files without needing to meet in person.

CBBS operated on a single computer connected to a phone

line, allowing users to dial in using a modem. Once connected, users could leave messages, upload or download files, and read bulletins posted by others. The system was simple but effective, and it quickly gained popularity among hobbyists and tech enthusiasts.

The Expansion of BBSs: Following the success of CBBS, the concept of BBSs spread rapidly. By the early 1980s, BBSs had proliferated across the United States and beyond, with thousands of systems operating in different cities and towns. Each BBS was typically run by an individual or a small group of enthusiasts, often referred to as "sysops" (system operators), who maintained the hardware and software, moderated discussions, and provided support to users.

The growth of BBSs was fueled by the increasing availability of personal computers and modems. As more people gained access to the necessary technology, they began setting up their own BBSs, catering to various interests and communities. BBSs became a popular way for people to connect with others who shared their hobbies, from computing and gaming to science fiction and ham radio.

The Evolution of BBS Software: In the early days of BBSs, the software used to run these systems was often custom-written by the sysops themselves. However, as the popularity of BBSs grew, several commercial and shareware BBS software packages were developed, making it easier for individuals to set up and maintain their own systems. Some of the most popular BBS software packages included:

- **RBBS-PC (Remote Bulletin Board System):** One of the earliest and most influential BBS software programs, RBBS-PC was released in 1982 and became widely used by hobbyists and small businesses.
- **Fido BBS:** Developed by Tom Jennings in 1984, Fido BBS was the software that eventually gave rise to FidoNet, one of the largest and most influential BBS

networks.

- **WWIV (World Wide Information Network):** WWIV was a popular BBS software package that allowed sysops to customize their systems extensively. It became known for its flexibility and the active community of users who contributed to its development.

The availability of these software packages democratized the creation of BBSs, allowing more people to participate in the burgeoning online community.

FidoNet and Other Prominent BBS Networks

The Emergence of FidoNet: FidoNet, created by Tom Jennings in 1984, was one of the most significant developments in the history of BBSs. FidoNet was a global network of BBSs that allowed users to exchange messages and files across different systems. This was a major advancement, as most BBSs at the time were isolated from one another, with users limited to interacting only with others who dialed into the same system.

FidoNet operated by using a "store and forward" system, where messages were routed from one BBS to another until they reached their destination. This method allowed users to communicate with people in different cities, states, and even countries, all through their local BBS. FidoNet quickly became a massive network, connecting thousands of BBSs around the world and facilitating the exchange of millions of messages each month.

Other Notable BBS Networks: While FidoNet was the most famous BBS network, several other networks also played important roles in the growth of the BBS community. Some of these included:

- **RelayNet (RIME):** RelayNet was a large BBS network that focused on discussion forums and message relays. It connected hundreds of BBSs and facilitated conversations on a wide range of topics, from technology and politics to hobbies and entertainment.

- **WWIVNet:** WWIVNet was a network of BBSs that used the WWIV software package. It was known for its strong community of developers and users who contributed to the ongoing development of the software and the network.
- **Fidonet-compatible networks:** Several other networks emerged that were compatible with the FidoNet protocol, allowing users to exchange messages and files across different networks. These included networks like OpusNet, EggNet, and others.

These networks played a crucial role in expanding the reach of BBSs and creating a sense of global community among users. They also provided a platform for the exchange of information, ideas, and culture, helping to shape the early internet.

How BBSs Functioned and What They Offered to Users

The Technical Operation of BBSs: At its core, a BBS was a computer system connected to a telephone line, which users could access remotely via a modem. When a user dialed into a BBS, they would connect to the system's terminal software, which provided a text-based interface for interacting with the system.

Once connected, users could perform a variety of tasks, depending on the features offered by the BBS. These typically included:

- **Message Boards:** BBSs often featured message boards or forums where users could post messages, respond to others, and engage in discussions on various topics. These forums were typically organized by subject matter, allowing users to find and participate in conversations that interested them.
- **File Sharing:** Many BBSs offered file libraries

where users could upload and download software, documents, images, and other digital content. This was a key feature of BBSs, as it allowed users to share resources and access new software and information.
- **Email and Private Messaging:** BBSs often included email and private messaging systems that allowed users to communicate directly with one another. This was an important feature for maintaining friendships and collaborations within the BBS community.
- **Games:** Many BBSs offered text-based games, known as "door games," that users could play during their sessions. These games ranged from simple puzzles to more complex role-playing games (RPGs) and were a popular pastime among BBS users.
- **Bulletin Boards and Announcements:** Sysops often used BBSs to post announcements, news, and updates relevant to the BBS community. This could include information about upcoming events, changes to the system, or important news stories.

The User Experience: Using a BBS was a unique experience that required a certain level of technical know-how. Users needed to understand how to operate a modem, configure their terminal software, and navigate the text-based interface of the BBS. Despite these challenges, the BBS community was known for being welcoming and supportive, with experienced users often helping newcomers get started.

For many users, logging into a BBS was a daily ritual. They would check for new messages, download the latest files, and catch up on the latest discussions in the forums. The asynchronous nature of BBS communication meant that users could participate in conversations at their own pace, responding to messages when it was convenient for them.

BBSs were also a source of entertainment and social interaction. The games, forums, and chat rooms offered a place for people to relax, have fun, and make new friends. For some, BBSs became a second home, where they could connect with like-minded individuals and escape the pressures of daily life.

The Cultural Impact of BBS Communities

Fostering Early Online Communities: BBSs were among the first platforms to foster online communities, where people could connect based on shared interests, hobbies, and goals. These communities were often tight-knit and deeply engaged, with users forming strong bonds with one another. The sense of camaraderie and belonging that BBSs provided was a key factor in their popularity and longevity.

The culture of BBSs was shaped by the values of their users and sysops. Many BBSs emphasized openness, collaboration, and mutual respect, creating a positive environment for discussion and learning. The early BBS community was also characterized by a strong sense of DIY (do-it-yourself) ethos, with users often taking an active role in the development and maintenance of the systems they used.

Influence on Modern Digital Communication: The influence of BBSs on modern digital communication is profound. Many of the features and norms that originated in BBS communities have carried over to today's online platforms. For example, the structure of message boards and forums on BBSs can be seen in modern discussion platforms like Reddit and online forums. The concept of file sharing, which was central to BBSs, laid the groundwork for peer-to-peer (P2P) networks and modern cloud storage services.

BBSs also played a role in the development of online identities and digital culture. Users often adopted pseudonyms or "handles" when participating in BBS communities, a practice that continues in many online spaces today. The culture of BBS **communities** also fostered early examples of internet subcultures, where groups of users with specific interests, from gaming to hacking, could find a space to connect and share knowledge. These subcultures would later evolve and expand as the internet itself grew, influencing everything from the development of software to the emergence of new artistic and cultural movements online.

The Role of BBSs in Political and Social Activism: BBSs were not just platforms for socializing and entertainment; they also became important tools for political and social activism. In the 1980s and 1990s, BBSs were used by various groups to organize, share information, and mobilize support for their causes. This included everything from local grassroots movements to international advocacy for human rights and free speech.

One of the most notable examples is the use of BBSs by the hacker collective "Cult of the Dead Cow," which used its platform to advocate for internet freedom and expose security vulnerabilities in major software systems. Similarly, environmental and anti-nuclear groups used BBSs to coordinate protests and share information that was often censored or ignored by mainstream media.

BBSs allowed activists to bypass traditional gatekeepers of information and communicate directly with like-minded individuals, regardless of geographical barriers. This ability to disseminate information quickly and efficiently made BBSs a powerful tool for social change and helped lay the groundwork for the digital activism that would become prevalent in the age of the internet.

The Decline of BBSs and Their Legacy: The rise of the World Wide Web in the mid-1990s marked the beginning of the decline for BBSs. As more people gained access to the internet through ISPs and web browsers, the need for dial-up BBSs diminished. The web offered a more user-friendly and visually rich environment, with greater accessibility and a broader range of content. Many BBSs either transitioned to web-based platforms or shut down entirely as their user base migrated to the internet.

However, the legacy of BBSs continues to influence the internet today. The principles of community-driven content, user-generated forums, and peer-to-peer interaction that were central to BBS culture can be seen in modern platforms such as social media networks, online forums, and collaborative projects like Wikipedia. The sense of online community and the emphasis on user empowerment that originated with BBSs are now fundamental aspects of the internet.

Additionally, the technical innovations developed within the BBS community, such as message threading, file sharing protocols, and user authentication methods, have been incorporated into a wide range of internet technologies. The pioneering spirit of the early BBS sysops and users paved the way for the participatory and decentralized nature of the modern internet.

Conclusion

The rise of Bulletin Board Systems (BBSs) represents a foundational chapter in the history of digital communication. These early online communities not only provided a platform for users to connect, share information, and collaborate but also set the stage for many of the social, cultural, and technical developments that would shape the future of the internet.

From the creation of the first BBS in 1978 to the emergence of global networks like FidoNet, BBSs were a breeding ground for innovation and community-building. They offered a unique blend of social interaction, information exchange, and entertainment, all within a digital space that was largely user-driven.

The cultural impact of BBSs is still felt today, as the principles of online community, user-generated content, and decentralized communication continue to influence the evolution of the internet. As we move forward in this book, we will explore how these early innovations laid the groundwork for the modern internet, including the development of web-based communities, social media, and the broader digital culture.

CHAPTER 5: THE DAWN OF GRAPHICAL USER INTERFACES (GUIS)

Overview

This chapter delves into the revolutionary development and popularization of graphical user interfaces (GUIs) that transformed personal computing from a niche activity for experts into an accessible tool for the general public. We will explore the shift from command-line interfaces (CLIs) to GUIs, the release of Windows 1.0 and its subsequent evolution, how GUIs democratized computing, and insights from developers and early users who witnessed this significant technological shift.

The Shift from Command-Line Interfaces to GUIs

The Era of Command-Line Interfaces: Before the advent of graphical user interfaces, computing was primarily conducted through command-line interfaces (CLIs), where users interacted with computers by typing text commands into a terminal. CLIs were powerful and flexible, allowing users to perform a wide range of tasks, from file management to programming. However, they were also challenging for the average person to use, as they required a deep understanding of specific commands and syntax.

For many years, CLIs were the standard for interacting with computers, particularly in professional and academic settings. However, as personal computing began to gain traction in the late 1970s and early 1980s, it became clear that a more user-friendly approach was needed to make computers accessible to a broader audience. The complexity of CLIs was a significant barrier for new users, limiting the appeal and potential of personal computers.

The Concept of a Graphical User Interface: The idea of a graphical user interface emerged as a solution to the limitations of CLIs. A GUI would allow users to interact with their computers using visual elements like icons, windows, and menus, rather than memorizing and typing commands. This approach promised to make computing more intuitive, reducing the learning curve and enabling more people to use computers effectively.

The concept of a GUI was first explored by researchers at Xerox PARC (Palo Alto Research Center) in the 1970s. The Xerox Alto, developed in 1973, was one of the first computers to feature a GUI. The Alto's interface included windows, icons, and a mouse-driven cursor, allowing users to manipulate digital objects on the screen in a way that mimicked physical interaction. Although the Alto was never commercially released, it had a profound influence on the future of personal computing.

The Release of Windows 1.0 and Its Evolution

Microsoft's Entry into the GUI Market: The release of Windows 1.0 in 1985 marked Microsoft's entry into the GUI market. Windows 1.0 was not an operating system in its own right, but rather a graphical shell that ran on top of MS-DOS, the dominant operating system of the time. It provided users with a visual interface that made it easier to navigate and manage their files, programs, and system settings.

Windows 1.0 featured several key elements that would become

standard in later versions, including overlapping windows, a menu bar, and the ability to use a mouse to interact with on-screen elements. However, it was limited in functionality and received mixed reviews upon its release. Many users found it slow and cumbersome compared to the command-line interface they were accustomed to.

The Evolution of Windows: Despite its initial shortcomings, Windows 1.0 laid the groundwork for future versions of the operating system. Over the next few years, Microsoft released several updates and new versions, each one improving on the last. Windows 2.0, released in 1987, introduced support for more sophisticated graphics and better multitasking capabilities. It also allowed application windows to overlap, a feature that became central to the Windows experience.

The real breakthrough came with the release of Windows 3.0 in 1990. This version featured a more refined interface, with improved performance, better memory management, and the introduction of the Program Manager and File Manager, which made it easier to organize and launch applications. Windows 3.0 was a commercial success, selling millions of copies and establishing Microsoft as a major player in the personal computing market.

The success of Windows 3.0 led to the release of Windows 3.1 in 1992, which added more features and improved stability. Windows 3.1 was also the first version to include TrueType fonts, making it possible to display text on the screen that matched printed output, a significant advancement for desktop publishing.

The Release of Windows 95: The culmination of Microsoft's efforts came with the release of Windows 95 in 1995. Windows 95 was a full-fledged operating system that integrated the graphical user interface with the underlying operating system, eliminating the need for MS-DOS as a separate environment. Windows 95 introduced the Start menu, taskbar, and a redesigned desktop, which became defining features of the

Windows interface.

Windows 95 also included support for long file names, built-in networking capabilities, and, crucially, a TCP/IP stack, which made it easier for users to connect to the growing internet. The release of Windows 95 was a cultural event, with a massive marketing campaign that included a promotional video featuring the Rolling Stones' song "Start Me Up." Windows 95 was a critical and commercial success, selling over 40 million copies in its first year and solidifying the GUI as the standard interface for personal computers.

How GUIs Made Computers More Accessible to the General Public

The Intuitive Nature of GUIs: The primary advantage of GUIs was their intuitiveness. By allowing users to interact with their computers using familiar visual metaphors, such as folders, trash bins, and desktops, GUIs made it easier for people to understand and use computers without needing extensive training. The use of a mouse to point and click on icons and menus eliminated the need to memorize complex commands, making computing more accessible to people with little or no technical background.

GUIs also enabled a more interactive and engaging experience. Users could see the immediate results of their actions on the screen, whether they were opening a file, launching a program, or moving a window. This direct manipulation of on-screen elements helped to demystify computing and made it feel more like a tool for creativity and productivity rather than a specialized technical instrument.

The Spread of GUIs Across Platforms: The success of Windows and other GUI-based operating systems, such as Apple's Macintosh, led to the widespread adoption of GUIs across different platforms. Apple's Macintosh, introduced in 1984, was the first commercially successful personal computer with a graphical user interface, and it played a significant role in popularizing the concept of a GUI.

The Mac's interface was user-friendly and visually appealing, featuring icons, menus, and a desktop that made it easy to navigate and use. The success of the Macintosh demonstrated the potential of GUIs to reach a broad audience, and it inspired other companies, including Microsoft, to develop their own GUI-based systems.

As GUIs became more common, software developers began designing applications specifically for these interfaces. This led to the creation of new categories of software, such as desktop publishing, graphic design, and multimedia, which took full advantage of the capabilities of GUIs. The growth of the software industry, in turn, drove the adoption of personal computers among businesses, schools, and households, making GUIs an integral part of daily life.

The Impact on Education and Accessibility: GUIs also had a profound impact on education and accessibility. The visual and interactive nature of GUIs made them an ideal tool for teaching computer literacy to students of all ages. Schools and universities began incorporating GUI-based computers into their curricula, helping to prepare a new generation of users for the digital age.

For individuals with disabilities, GUIs offered new opportunities for interaction and communication. Features such as screen readers, on-screen keyboards, and customizable interfaces made it possible for people with visual, motor, or cognitive impairments to use computers more effectively. The development of assistive technologies, combined with the flexibility of GUIs, contributed to the digital inclusion of people with disabilities.

Interviews with Developers and Users of Early GUIs

Insights from Developers: To gain a deeper understanding of the development and impact of GUIs, we spoke with several key figures who were involved in their creation. Among them was Bill Atkinson, one of the principal designers of the Macintosh

GUI at Apple. Atkinson recalled the early challenges of designing an interface that was both powerful and easy to use. "We wanted to create something that felt natural, something that people could just pick up and start using without needing a manual," Atkinson explained. "It was about bringing the power of computing to everyone, not just the experts."

Similarly, Brad Silverberg, a senior executive at Microsoft during the development of Windows 95, emphasized the importance of user feedback in shaping the GUI. "We spent countless hours testing and refining the interface, listening to what users wanted and making sure the experience was as smooth and intuitive as possible," Silverberg said. "The goal was to make the computer an extension of the user's own abilities."

Experiences of Early Users: We also spoke with several early users of GUI-based systems, who shared their memories of transitioning from command-line interfaces to graphical interfaces. Janet Hughes, a graphic designer who started using the Macintosh in the mid-1980s, described how the GUI revolutionized her work. "Before the Mac, everything was done by hand, with rulers and paper. The Mac changed all that. Suddenly, I could experiment with layouts, fonts, and colors on the screen, and it was incredibly liberating," Hughes said.

Similarly, James Lawson, a small business owner who adopted Windows 3.0 for his office in 1990, recalled the impact of the GUI on his operations. "Windows made it possible for me to manage my business more efficiently. I didn't need to hire a full-time tech person because the interface was so easy to understand. It was a game-changer," Lawson explained.

These interviews highlight the transformative effect that **GUIs had on both the development of technology and the everyday lives of users.** The shift from command-line interfaces to graphical user interfaces not only made computers more accessible but also empowered a broader range of people to use technology in creative and productive ways. The stories from developers and early users illustrate how GUIs democratized computing, making it possible for more people to harness the power of computers without needing to be technical experts.

The Cultural Impact of GUIs: The cultural impact of GUIs cannot be overstated. By making computers more accessible, GUIs played a significant role in the spread of personal computing during the 1980s and 1990s. This, in turn, contributed to the rise of the digital age, where computers became an essential tool for work, education, and entertainment.

The popularization of GUIs also influenced the design of other technologies, from smartphones to gaming consoles, which adopted similar principles to make their interfaces more user-friendly. The success of GUIs in personal computing helped to establish the importance of user-centered design in technology, a philosophy that continues to guide the development of new products and services today.

The Legacy of Early GUIs: The legacy of early graphical user interfaces is evident in the modern computing environment. The basic principles of GUI design—such as windows, icons, menus, and pointers—remain central to most operating systems and software applications. The ideas pioneered by early GUI developers at companies like Xerox, Apple, and Microsoft laid the foundation for the interactive, visually-rich interfaces we use today.

Moreover, the shift to GUIs paved the way for the broader adoption of personal computers in homes and businesses around the world. By lowering the barrier to entry, GUIs made it possible for millions of people to participate in the digital revolution, contributing to the rapid growth of the tech industry and the global economy.

Conclusion

The dawn of graphical user interfaces marked a turning point in the history of computing, transforming the way people interact with technology and making computers accessible to the masses. From the early experiments at Xerox PARC to the release of Windows 1.0 and the evolution of the Macintosh, GUIs revolutionized personal computing by replacing the complexity of command-line interfaces with intuitive, visual interactions.

The development of GUIs was not just a technical achievement; it was a cultural one as well. By making computing more approachable, GUIs empowered people from all walks of life to use technology in their work, education, and daily lives. The interviews with developers and early users highlight the profound impact that GUIs had on the personal and professional lives of millions of people.

As we continue to explore the history of the internet and computing, it is clear that the development of GUIs was a critical step in the journey toward the interconnected, digital world we live in today. The principles of GUI design continue to shape the evolution of technology, ensuring that computers remain accessible, user-friendly, and integral to our modern lives.

CHAPTER 6: WINDOWS 95: THE GAME CHANGER

Overview

This chapter explores the release of Windows 95, a monumental event in the history of personal computing and the mainstream adoption of the internet. We will delve into the integration of the TCP/IP stack into Windows 95, the introduction of key features like the Start menu, taskbar, and Internet Explorer, the innovative marketing strategies that propelled Windows 95 to success, and first-hand accounts of the launch and its impact on users and the technology industry.

The Integration of the TCP/IP Stack into Windows 95

The Importance of TCP/IP Integration: One of the most significant advancements in Windows 95 was the integration of the TCP/IP protocol stack directly into the operating system. Before Windows 95, configuring a computer to connect to the internet required installing and configuring separate networking software, a process that was often complex and daunting for average users. The inclusion of TCP/IP in Windows 95 simplified this process, making it much easier for users to connect to the internet.

The Transmission Control Protocol/Internet Protocol (TCP/IP) is the foundational protocol suite for the internet, responsible for ensuring that data packets are transmitted reliably across networks. By integrating TCP/IP natively into Windows 95, Microsoft ensured that users could access the internet with minimal setup, paving the way for the rapid expansion of internet connectivity in homes and businesses.

Impact on Internet Adoption: The seamless integration of TCP/IP into Windows 95 played a crucial role in the widespread adoption of the internet during the mid-1990s. With the launch of Windows 95, millions of users who had previously been intimidated by the complexity of networking suddenly found it easy to get online. This ease of access helped accelerate the growth of the World Wide Web, as more people began exploring online resources, communicating via email, and participating in online communities.

For many users, Windows 95 was their first experience with the internet. The operating system's built-in support for TCP/IP meant that connecting to the internet was as simple as plugging in a modem and configuring a few settings. This user-friendly approach demystified the process of getting online and contributed to the explosive growth of internet users in the latter half of the 1990s.

The Introduction of the Start Menu, Taskbar, and Internet Explorer

The Start Menu and Taskbar: Revolutionizing User Interaction: Windows 95 introduced several key features that fundamentally changed the way users interacted with their computers. The most iconic of these was the Start menu, a centralized location for accessing programs, files, and system settings. The Start menu provided users with a simple and intuitive way to navigate their computer, replacing the cluttered Program Manager of previous Windows versions with a more organized and efficient interface.

Alongside the Start menu, Windows 95 introduced the taskbar, a horizontal strip at the bottom of the screen that displayed open windows and running applications. The taskbar made it easier for users to switch between tasks, monitor active programs, and manage their workspace. Together, the Start menu and taskbar transformed the user experience, making it easier to perform everyday tasks and access the tools needed for work and entertainment.

Internet Explorer: Microsoft's Foray into Web Browsing: Another groundbreaking feature of Windows 95 was the inclusion of Internet Explorer, Microsoft's first web browser. Internet Explorer was initially offered as an optional add-on with the Windows 95 Plus! Pack, but it was soon bundled directly with the operating system. This move marked Microsoft's entry into the web browser market, setting the stage for the "browser wars" that would dominate the tech industry in the years to come.

Internet Explorer made it easier for users to explore the World Wide Web, offering a user-friendly interface for browsing websites, sending emails, and downloading content. The browser's integration with Windows 95 meant that users could access the internet directly from their desktop, further simplifying the process of getting online.

Impact on User Behavior and Software Development: The introduction of the Start menu, taskbar, and Internet Explorer had a profound impact on user behavior and the development of software. These features made personal computers more accessible and user-friendly, encouraging a wider audience to embrace technology in their daily lives. The ease of use and intuitive design of Windows 95 set a new standard for operating systems, influencing the development of software across the industry.

For software developers, Windows 95 offered a more stable and feature-rich platform for creating applications. The operating system's support for long file names, multitasking, and a standardized graphical user interface (GUI) allowed developers to create more sophisticated and user-friendly software. This, in turn, fueled the growth of the software industry and expanded the range of applications available to consumers.

Marketing Strategies That Led to Windows 95's Success

The "Start Me Up" Campaign: The launch of Windows 95 was accompanied by one of the most ambitious and high-profile marketing campaigns in the history of technology. Microsoft invested over $300 million in a global advertising blitz that featured the Rolling Stones' song "Start Me Up" as its anthem. The campaign was designed to generate excitement and anticipation for Windows 95, positioning it as a revolutionary product that would change the way people used computers.

The "Start Me Up" campaign was notable not only for its scale but also for its focus on mainstream audiences. Microsoft's marketing efforts targeted a broad demographic, emphasizing the accessibility and ease of use of Windows 95. Television commercials, print ads, and even a 30-minute infomercial featuring comedian Jennifer Aniston and actor Matthew Perry were used to introduce the public to the new features of Windows 95.

Retail and Promotional Strategies: In addition to its advertising campaign, Microsoft employed several innovative retail and promotional strategies to ensure the success of Windows 95. The company partnered with major retailers to create elaborate in-store displays and launch events, turning the release of Windows 95 into a cultural phenomenon. Midnight launch events were held at stores around the world, with lines of customers eagerly waiting to purchase the new operating system.

Microsoft also collaborated with hardware manufacturers to bundle Windows 95 with new computers, ensuring that the operating system would reach a wide audience from day one. This strategy helped to solidify Windows 95 as the default choice for personal computing, as millions of new PCs shipped with the operating system pre-installed.

The Role of the Media and Public Relations: The media played a crucial role in building anticipation for Windows 95. Microsoft's public relations team worked tirelessly to generate coverage in newspapers, magazines, and television programs. The operating system was featured on the cover of major publications, and tech journalists provided extensive reviews and analyses of its features.

The hype surrounding Windows 95 extended beyond the tech world, with coverage in mainstream media outlets that highlighted the operating system's potential to transform everyday life. This widespread media attention helped to create a sense of urgency and excitement, driving record sales and establishing Windows 95 as a cultural touchstone.

First-Hand Accounts of the Windows 95 Launch and Its Reception

The Launch Event: A Global Phenomenon: The launch of Windows 95 on August 24, 1995, was a global event that captured the attention of both the tech industry and the general public. In Redmond, Washington, Microsoft hosted a massive launch party attended by thousands of employees, partners, and members of the media. The event featured a live performance by Jay Leno and a countdown to the official release of the operating system.

Around the world, stores opened their doors at midnight to eager customers who lined up to be among the first to purchase Windows 95. In some cities, the demand was so high that stores sold out of copies within hours. The launch was covered extensively by news outlets, with live broadcasts and reports capturing the excitement of the moment.

Reactions from Users and Industry Experts: The reception to Windows 95 was overwhelmingly positive, with users and industry experts praising the operating system for its ease of use, stability, and innovative features. For many users, Windows 95 represented a significant leap forward in personal computing, making it easier to perform everyday tasks and connect to the internet.

One early adopter, Sarah Thompson, described her experience with Windows 95 as "transformative." "I had been using DOS and Windows 3.1 for years, but Windows 95 was something completely different. The Start menu and taskbar made everything so much easier to find, and getting online was a breeze. It felt like the future had finally arrived," she said.

Tech journalists and analysts were also impressed with the operating system. John C. Dvorak, a prominent technology columnist, wrote that Windows 95 was "a watershed moment in the history of personal computing," while others praised its user-friendly interface and robust networking capabilities. The operating system's ability to seamlessly integrate with the internet was seen as a major advancement, positioning Windows 95 as the ideal platform for the emerging digital age.

Challenges and Criticisms: Despite the widespread acclaim, Windows 95 was not without its challenges and criticisms. Some users reported issues with hardware compatibility, particularly with older peripherals that were not supported by the new operating system. Additionally, while Windows 95 was more stable than its predecessors, it was still prone to crashes and system errors, particularly when running multiple applications simultaneously.

Critics also pointed to the aggressive marketing tactics used by Microsoft, arguing that the company's dominance in the operating system market stifled competition. The bundling of Internet Explorer with Windows 95 became a particularly contentious issue, leading to antitrust investigations and legal challenges in the years that followed.

However, these criticisms did little to dampen the overall success of Windows 95. The operating system sold more than 40 million copies in its first year, making it one of the best-selling software products of all time. Its impact on the personal computing industry was profound, setting new standards for usability, functionality, and internet connectivity.

Conclusion

The release of Windows 95 was a game-changer in every **sense of the word.** It marked a turning point in the history of personal computing, transforming the way people interacted with their computers and accelerating the mainstream adoption of the internet. The integration of the TCP/IP stack, the introduction of the Start menu, taskbar, and Internet Explorer, and the innovative marketing strategies all contributed to the operating system's enormous success.

Windows 95 not only made computers more accessible and user-friendly but also played a crucial role in bringing the internet into millions of homes around the world. By simplifying the process of getting online, Windows 95 helped to demystify the internet and encourage a new wave of users to explore the World Wide Web, communicate via email, and participate in the emerging digital economy.

The operating system's launch was a cultural phenomenon, capturing the imagination of the public and solidifying Microsoft's position as a dominant force in the technology industry. The excitement and anticipation surrounding the release of Windows 95 were unprecedented, and the operating system's success set the stage for the rapid expansion of the personal computing market in the years that followed.

Looking back, it's clear that Windows 95 was more than just an operating system; it was a catalyst for change, driving the adoption of new technologies and shaping the future of computing. Its legacy can be seen in the continued evolution of Windows, the growth of the internet, and the widespread use of graphical user interfaces that have become a standard in modern computing.

As we move forward in this book, we will continue to explore the impact of these technological advancements on the development of the internet and the broader digital landscape, tracing the journey from the early days of personal computing to the interconnected world we live in today.

CHAPTER 7: THE BACKBONE OF THE INTERNET: TCP/IP STACKS

Overview

This chapter delves into the technical intricacies of the Transmission Control Protocol/Internet Protocol (TCP/IP) suite and its fundamental role in connecting the world. We will explore the detailed components of the TCP/IP protocol suite, how TCP/IP stacks facilitate data communication, the evolution of TCP/IP from academic networks to commercial use, and the critical importance of TCP/IP in the modern internet infrastructure.

A Detailed Explanation of the TCP/IP Protocol Suite

The Origins of TCP/IP: The TCP/IP protocol suite was developed in the early 1970s as part of a project funded by the United States Department of Defense. The goal was to create a robust and scalable networking protocol that could facilitate communication across diverse and geographically dispersed networks. Vint Cerf and Bob Kahn, two pioneers in the field of computer networking, are credited with designing TCP/IP, which has since become the backbone of the global internet.

The Structure of the TCP/IP Protocol Suite: The TCP/IP protocol suite is organized into four layers, each responsible for different aspects of data communication. These layers, from highest to lowest, are the Application Layer, the Transport Layer, the Internet Layer, and the Link Layer. Each layer builds upon the functions of the one below it, allowing for modularity and flexibility in networking.

1. **Application Layer:**
   - The Application Layer is the topmost layer of the TCP/IP protocol suite, responsible for providing network services directly to end-user applications. Protocols at this layer include Hypertext Transfer Protocol (HTTP), File Transfer Protocol (FTP), Simple Mail Transfer Protocol (SMTP), and Domain Name System (DNS). This layer enables applications to communicate over the network by using standardized protocols, facilitating activities like web browsing, email, and file sharing.

2. **Transport Layer:**
   - The Transport Layer is responsible for ensuring reliable data transmission between devices on a network. The two primary protocols in this layer are Transmission Control Protocol (TCP) and User Datagram Protocol (UDP). TCP is a connection-oriented protocol that guarantees the delivery of data in the correct order, with mechanisms for error checking and flow control. UDP, on the other hand, is a connectionless protocol that offers faster transmission by sacrificing reliability, making it suitable for applications like video streaming and online gaming.

3. **Internet Layer:**
   - The Internet Layer is responsible for routing

data packets across networks, ensuring that they reach their intended destination. The primary protocol at this layer is the Internet Protocol (IP), which assigns unique IP addresses to devices on the network and manages the forwarding of packets from one network to another. The Internet Layer also includes protocols like Internet Control Message Protocol (ICMP) and Address Resolution Protocol (ARP), which assist in network management and address mapping.

4. **Link Layer:**

    - The Link Layer, also known as the Network Interface Layer, is responsible for the physical transmission of data over network media, such as Ethernet cables or wireless signals. This layer includes protocols and technologies like Ethernet, Wi-Fi, and Point-to-Point Protocol (PPP), which define how data is formatted for transmission and how network devices interact with the physical network infrastructure.

How TCP/IP Operates: When a user sends data over a network, such as an email or a web request, the data is first broken down into smaller units called packets. These packets are then passed through each layer of the TCP/IP protocol stack, with each layer adding its own header information to ensure proper routing, delivery, and reassembly.

- **At the Application Layer:** The data is prepared for transmission by the application protocol, such as HTTP or SMTP, which defines the format and structure of the data.

- **At the Transport Layer:** The data is segmented into smaller packets, and the TCP or UDP protocol adds a header that includes information like port numbers

and sequence numbers (for TCP).
- **At the Internet Layer:** The packets are assigned IP addresses, which allow them to be routed across different networks. The IP header also includes information about the source and destination addresses.
- **At the Link Layer:** The packets are converted into frames suitable for transmission over the physical network medium. The frames are then transmitted to the next device on the network, such as a router or switch.

At the receiving end, the process is reversed, with each layer stripping away its corresponding header and reassembling the data before delivering it to the application.

How TCP/IP Stacks Facilitate Data Communication

The Role of TCP/IP Stacks in Data Transmission: A TCP/IP stack is a collection of software protocols that implement the functions of the TCP/IP protocol suite within a device, such as a computer, smartphone, or router. The stack handles all the tasks involved in sending and receiving data over a network, from breaking down data into packets to reassembling them at the destination.

Connection Establishment and Management: For TCP, which is a connection-oriented protocol, data communication begins with the establishment of a connection between the sender and the receiver. This process is known as the "three-way handshake," which involves three steps:

1. **SYN:** The sender sends a SYN (synchronize) packet to the receiver to initiate a connection.
2. **SYN-ACK:** The receiver responds with a SYN-ACK (synchronize-acknowledge) packet, acknowledging the connection request.
3. **ACK:** The sender sends an ACK (acknowledge) packet

to confirm the connection, and data transmission can begin.

Once the connection is established, TCP manages the flow of data, ensuring that packets are delivered in sequence, retransmitting any that are lost, and adjusting the transmission rate based on network conditions. This reliability is crucial for applications like web browsing, file transfers, and email, where data integrity is essential.

Routing and Forwarding: The Internet Protocol (IP) within the TCP/IP stack is responsible for routing packets from the source to the destination. Each packet contains the IP address of its destination, and as it travels across the network, routers read this address to determine the best path for the packet to take. This process, known as forwarding, involves routers passing the packet from one network to another until it reaches its final destination.

IP is designed to handle the complexities of a global network, where packets may need to traverse multiple networks, each with its own characteristics. The protocol's ability to route packets dynamically, based on network topology and conditions, is what allows the internet to scale and accommodate billions of devices worldwide.

Error Detection and Correction: TCP/IP includes mechanisms for error detection and correction, ensuring that data is transmitted accurately over the network. TCP uses checksums to detect errors in transmitted packets, and if an error is detected, the protocol can request the retransmission of the affected packet. This error-checking process is essential for maintaining data integrity, particularly over unreliable or congested networks.

The Evolution of TCP/IP from Academic Networks to Commercial Use

Academic and Military Origins: TCP/IP was initially developed as part of the ARPANET project, funded by the U.S. Department of Defense's Advanced Research Projects Agency (ARPA). ARPANET was designed to be a resilient and decentralized network that could withstand disruptions, making it an ideal platform for research and military communication. The success of ARPANET demonstrated the viability of packet-switched networking and laid the foundation for the development of TCP/IP.

In the 1970s and early 1980s, TCP/IP was primarily used within academic and research institutions, where it facilitated communication and collaboration between researchers. The protocol's flexibility and robustness made it well-suited for these environments, where diverse networks needed to be connected seamlessly.

Adoption by the National Science Foundation (NSF): The turning point for TCP/IP came in the mid-1980s, when the National Science Foundation (NSF) adopted the protocol for its NSFNET project. NSFNET was a high-speed network that connected supercomputing centers and research institutions across the United States, serving as a backbone for academic networking.

NSF's decision to use TCP/IP as the standard protocol for NSFNET was instrumental in its widespread adoption. As more academic institutions joined NSFNET, they were required to use TCP/IP, which led to the protocol becoming the de facto standard for academic and research networks. This adoption also helped to establish TCP/IP as a global standard, as other countries and institutions followed NSF's lead.

The Transition to Commercial Use: By the late 1980s and early 1990s, the commercial potential of TCP/IP was becoming increasingly evident. The rise of the internet as a global communication platform created demand for a protocol that could support a wide range of applications, from email to web browsing to online commerce. TCP/IP, with its proven track record in academic and research settings, was ideally suited for this role.

The commercialization of the internet in the 1990s led to the widespread adoption of TCP/IP by businesses, governments, and individuals. Internet Service Providers (ISPs) began offering TCP/IP-based internet access to the public, and companies started building networks that used TCP/IP to connect their offices, employees, and customers. This transition was further accelerated by the release of user-friendly operating systems like Windows 95, which integrated TCP/IP natively, making it easier for non-technical users to connect to the internet.

Global Standardization: As TCP/IP became the standard for commercial and public networks, it was formalized through international standards organizations like the Internet Engineering Task Force (IETF) and the International Organization for Standardization (ISO). These organizations developed and maintained the specifications for TCP/IP, ensuring that the protocol remained interoperable and scalable as the internet continued to grow.

The global standardization of TCP/IP allowed the internet to expand rapidly, connecting networks and devices around the world. Today, TCP/IP is the foundational protocol for the internet, used by billions of devices to communicate across a global network.

The Importance of TCP /IP in the Modern Internet Infrastructure

The Ubiquity of TCP/IP: Today, TCP/IP is the fundamental protocol suite that underpins the entire internet. Virtually all online communication, from browsing the web to sending emails, streaming videos, and conducting financial transactions, relies on TCP/IP. The protocol's design allows it to operate seamlessly across diverse hardware and software platforms, making it the universal standard for network communication.

The ubiquity of TCP/IP has made it the common language of

the internet, enabling devices ranging from smartphones and laptops to servers and IoT (Internet of Things) devices to communicate effectively. This universal adoption ensures that networks across the globe can interconnect, creating a truly global and interoperable network.

Scalability and Flexibility: One of the key strengths of TCP/IP is its scalability. The protocol was designed to accommodate a growing number of devices and networks, making it capable of scaling from the small, experimental ARPANET to the modern internet, which connects billions of devices. TCP/IP's layered architecture allows new technologies to be integrated without disrupting existing networks, ensuring that the internet can evolve and expand over time.

The flexibility of TCP/IP also allows it to support a wide range of applications and services. Whether it's high-bandwidth applications like video streaming or low-latency requirements for online gaming, TCP/IP can handle diverse demands while maintaining reliable communication. This adaptability has been crucial in the development of new internet technologies and services.

Security and Reliability: Security has become a critical concern in the modern internet landscape, and TCP/IP has evolved to address these challenges. While the original design of TCP/IP did not include robust security features, the protocol suite has been extended with additional layers and protocols to enhance security. For example, protocols like Secure Sockets Layer (SSL) and its successor, Transport Layer Security (TLS), provide encryption and authentication for web traffic, protecting data from eavesdropping and tampering.

In addition to security, TCP/IP is known for its reliability. TCP, in particular, ensures that data is delivered accurately and in the correct order, making it ideal for applications where data integrity is paramount. The protocol's ability to detect and retransmit lost packets helps maintain reliable communication even over unstable networks.

The Foundation for Future Technologies: As new technologies emerge, TCP/IP continues to play a central role in their development and deployment. The ongoing transition to IPv6, the latest version of the Internet Protocol, is a key example of how TCP/IP is evolving to meet the demands of a growing internet. IPv6 addresses the limitations of IPv4, particularly the shortage of available IP addresses, by providing a vastly larger address space. This transition is critical for the continued expansion of the internet, particularly as the number of connected devices continues to rise.

Moreover, TCP/IP remains at the core of other emerging technologies, such as cloud computing, 5G networks, and the Internet of Things (IoT). These technologies rely on the robust and flexible nature of TCP/IP to deliver new services and capabilities to users around the world.

The Role of TCP/IP in Internet Governance: TCP/IP is not just a technical standard; it is also a key component of internet governance. Organizations like the Internet Engineering Task Force (IETF) and the Internet Corporation for Assigned Names and Numbers (ICANN) oversee the development and management of TCP/IP standards, ensuring that the internet remains open, interoperable, and scalable. These organizations play a crucial role in maintaining the stability and security of the global internet, and their work ensures that TCP/IP continues to serve as the foundation for digital communication.

Global Impact and Future Outlook: The impact of TCP/IP on the modern world cannot be overstated. It has enabled the creation of the internet as we know it, transforming how we communicate, conduct business, and access information. The protocol's ability to connect diverse networks and devices has made it possible for people around the world to interact and collaborate in ways that were previously unimaginable.

As we look to the future, TCP/IP will continue to be a cornerstone of the digital age. Its ongoing evolution will support the development of new technologies, from artificial intelligence to quantum computing, ensuring that the internet remains a dynamic and vital platform for innovation. The resilience and adaptability of TCP/IP will allow it to meet the challenges of an increasingly connected world, securing its place as the backbone of the internet for decades to come.

Conclusion

The TCP/IP protocol suite is the bedrock upon which the modern internet is built. From its origins in academic and military research to its widespread adoption in commercial networks, TCP/IP has proven to be a robust, scalable, and flexible framework for global communication. Its ability to facilitate reliable data transmission across diverse networks has made it the universal standard for internet connectivity.

The integration of TCP/IP into operating systems like Windows 95 played a critical role in bringing the internet to the masses, while its ongoing evolution continues to support the rapid growth and diversification of online services. As the internet continues to expand and new technologies emerge, TCP/IP will remain at the heart of the digital revolution, connecting people, devices, and networks around the world.

In the chapters to come, we will explore how these foundational technologies have paved the way for the explosive growth of the internet, the rise of the World Wide Web, and the development of new forms of digital communication and collaboration.

CHAPTER 8: EARLY ONLINE SERVICES: PIONEERS OF THE DIGITAL AGE

Overview

This chapter explores the pioneering online services of the 1980s and 1990s, such as CompuServe, America Online (AOL), Delphi, and The WELL, which played a crucial role in shaping modern internet usage. These early services provided users with access to email, forums, chat rooms, and information long before the World Wide Web became widely accessible. We will examine the founding and growth of these services, their impact on internet adoption, the unique culture and community they fostered, and personal stories from users and employees who experienced the early days of online connectivity.

The Founding and Growth of CompuServe

The Birth of CompuServe: CompuServe, founded in 1969 by Jeffrey Wilkins and Dr. John Goltz, was one of the first major online services available to the public. Originally established as a computer time-sharing service, CompuServe quickly evolved into a consumer-oriented online service that offered users a variety of features, including email, forums, file sharing, and news services.

CompuServe initially targeted business professionals, providing them with access to remote computing resources and information databases. However, as personal computers became more prevalent in the late 1970s and early 1980s, CompuServe shifted its focus to the consumer market, offering a subscription-based service that allowed users to connect to its network via a modem and telephone line.

The Expansion of Services: Throughout the 1980s, CompuServe continued to expand its offerings, becoming a comprehensive online service with a wide range of features that appealed to both businesses and individual users. Some of the key services offered by CompuServe included:

- **Email:** CompuServe was one of the first online services to offer email, allowing users to send and receive messages with others on the network. This feature quickly became one of the most popular aspects of the service, revolutionizing the way people communicated.
- **Forums and Discussion Groups:** CompuServe hosted a variety of forums and discussion groups on topics ranging from technology and science to hobbies and entertainment. These forums allowed users to connect with others who shared their interests and engage in discussions on a wide range of subjects.
- **News and Information:** CompuServe provided users with access to news services, including Reuters and The Associated Press, offering up-to-date information on current events, finance, and more.
- **File Sharing:** Users could upload and download software, documents, and other files through CompuServe's file-sharing service. This feature was particularly popular among computer enthusiasts and programmers who wanted to share their work with

others.

The Impact on Early Internet Adoption: CompuServe played a significant role in introducing the general public to the concept of online connectivity. By offering a wide range of services and an easy-to-use interface, CompuServe made it possible for people with little technical expertise to access the online world. The service's popularity grew rapidly, and by the mid-1980s, CompuServe had become the largest online service in the United States, with hundreds of thousands of subscribers.

CompuServe's influence extended beyond its user base, as it also played a key role in shaping the development of the internet. The service's email system, for example, was one of the first to implement the now-standard @ symbol in email addresses, setting the precedent for email formatting that is still used today.

AOL's Rise to Dominance in the Online Services Market

The Founding of AOL: America Online (AOL) was founded in 1985 by Steve Case, Jim Kimsey, and Marc Seriff as Quantum Computer Services. Originally, the company provided an online service called "Q-Link" for Commodore 64 users, offering access to games, chat rooms, and email. However, it wasn't until the company rebranded as America Online in 1989 and began targeting a broader audience that it truly began to take off.

AOL's mission was to make online services accessible to the masses. To achieve this, the company focused on creating a user-friendly interface that required no technical expertise to navigate. AOL's interface featured a graphical design with icons and menus, making it easy for users to access the service's features without needing to memorize complex commands.

The Expansion of AOL's Services: Throughout the 1990s, AOL expanded its services and rapidly grew its subscriber base. Some of the key features that contributed to AOL's success included:

- **Easy-to-Use Interface:** AOL's graphical user interface

(GUI) was designed to be intuitive and accessible, making it easy for users to navigate the service's offerings. This focus on usability helped AOL attract a broad audience, including families and individuals who had little experience with computers.

- **Chat Rooms and Instant Messaging:** AOL's chat rooms and instant messaging services were some of its most popular features. Users could join chat rooms on a wide variety of topics, from hobbies to current events, and engage in real-time conversations with others. AOL's instant messaging service, known as "AIM" (AOL Instant Messenger), became a cultural phenomenon, allowing users to communicate with friends and family instantly.

- **Content and Media Partnerships:** AOL partnered with a variety of media companies to offer exclusive content to its users, including news, entertainment, and educational resources. These partnerships helped to differentiate AOL from other online services and attracted users who were interested in accessing premium content.

- **Free Trial CDs:** One of AOL's most successful marketing strategies was its distribution of free trial CDs. These CDs, which were sent through the mail or included with computer magazines, offered users a free trial of AOL's services. The widespread distribution of these CDs helped AOL rapidly expand its subscriber base, making it one of the most recognized brands in the online services market.

AOL's Dominance and Cultural Impact: By the mid-1990s, AOL had become the largest online service provider in the United States, with millions of subscribers. The company's success was driven by its focus on accessibility, user-friendly design, and aggressive marketing. AOL became synonymous with the internet for many people, and its "You've Got Mail" notification became an iconic sound of the digital age.

AOL's impact on digital culture was profound. The service introduced millions of people to the online world and helped to popularize features like email, chat rooms, and instant messaging. AOL also played a significant role in the commercialization of the internet, pioneering the use of online advertising and subscription-based services.

However, AOL's dominance began to wane in the early 2000s as broadband internet became more widely available and users migrated to web-based services. Despite this decline, AOL's legacy as a pioneer of the digital age remains significant, and the company's influence can still be seen in the modern internet landscape.

Delphi's Contribution to Internet Access for Users

The Founding of Delphi: Delphi, founded in 1981 by Wes Kussmaul, was another early online service that played a crucial role in expanding access to the internet. Originally launched as a text-based information service, Delphi offered its users access to databases, news, and discussion forums. Over time, Delphi evolved to become one of the first services to provide internet access to the general public.

In 1992, Delphi became the first national commercial online service to offer access to the World Wide Web, allowing its users to browse websites and use internet-based email. This move was a significant milestone in the history of the internet, as it marked the beginning of the transition from proprietary online services to the open internet.

Delphi's Role in Internet Adoption: Delphi's decision to offer internet access was driven by the recognition that the World Wide Web was rapidly becoming the dominant platform for online communication and information sharing. By providing users with access to the internet, Delphi helped to bridge the gap between the closed, proprietary networks of the early online services and the open, decentralized internet that we know today.

Delphi's users were among the first to experience the web as we now understand it, with the ability to browse websites, send emails, and participate in online communities on a global scale. This early exposure to the internet helped to create a generation of internet-savvy users who would go on to shape the development of the digital world.

Challenges and Legacy: Despite its pioneering role, Delphi faced significant challenges in competing with larger online services like CompuServe and AOL. The company struggled to maintain its subscriber base as the internet became more mainstream, and by the mid-1990s, Delphi had largely been overshadowed by its competitors.

However, Delphi's legacy as a trailblazer in internet access remains significant. The service's early adoption of the World Wide Web and its commitment to providing users with open internet access helped to set the stage for the widespread adoption of the internet in the years that followed. Delphi's impact can still be felt today in the way that online services and internet access are structured.

The Unique Culture and Community of The WELL

The Founding of The WELL: The Whole Earth 'Lectronic Link (The WELL) was founded in 1985 by Stewart Brand and Larry Brilliant as an online community for members of the Whole Earth Catalog, a publication that focused on counterculture, environmentalism, and technology. The WELL was unique in that it was designed to be a community-driven platform where users could engage in deep, thoughtful discussions on a wide range of topics.

The WELL operated as a text-based BBS (Bulletin Board System), where users could join conferences (forums) on various subjects, from technology and politics to philosophy and the arts. The platform was known for its strong emphasis on free speech, intellectual debate, and a sense of community.

The Culture of The WELL: The WELL quickly gained a reputation as a haven for creative thinkers, writers, and technologists. The community attracted a diverse group of users, **including influential figures from the world of technology, journalism, and the arts.** Members of The WELL often used their real names rather than pseudonyms, fostering a sense of accountability and encouraging thoughtful, respectful discourse. This was a stark contrast to many other online forums of the time, where anonymity often led to less constructive interactions.

The culture of The WELL was heavily influenced by the values of the Whole Earth Catalog, which emphasized self-reliance, curiosity, and a commitment to improving the world. Discussions on The WELL ranged from the practical to the philosophical, with users sharing knowledge, debating ideas, and supporting one another in their personal and professional lives. The community was also known for its openness to new ideas and its embrace of the "hacker ethic," which valued transparency, collaboration, and the free exchange of information.

The WELL's Influence on Online Communities: The WELL is often credited with pioneering many of the concepts that have since become fundamental to online communities. For example, the platform's emphasis on user-generated content and its reliance on a strong sense of community set the stage for the development of social media and online forums. The WELL's approach to moderation, which was largely driven by the community itself rather than by top-down control, also influenced the way that many later online communities were managed.

The WELL was particularly influential in the early days of the internet, as it provided a model for how online spaces could foster meaningful connections and discussions. Its members included notable figures such as Howard Rheingold, who wrote extensively about the concept of virtual communities, and John

Perry Barlow, who later co-founded the Electronic Frontier Foundation (EFF), an organization dedicated to defending digital civil liberties.

The WELL's Legacy: Although The WELL never achieved the massive scale of services like AOL or CompuServe, its impact on the development of online culture was profound. The platform demonstrated the potential for online communities to be more than just places for casual interaction—they could be spaces where people came together to share knowledge, collaborate on projects, and engage in deep, meaningful discussions.

Even today, The WELL is regarded as a pioneering experiment in online community-building, and its influence can be seen in the design and culture of many modern digital platforms. The values of openness, transparency, and community engagement that were central to The WELL continue to resonate in the digital world, particularly in the growing emphasis on creating positive, supportive online environments.

Personal Stories from Users and Employees of These Services

Stories from CompuServe Users: For many early adopters, CompuServe was their first experience with the online world. Susan Meyers, a longtime CompuServe user, recalls how the service changed her approach to research and communication. "I was a librarian, and CompuServe opened up a whole new world for me," she said. "Suddenly, I had access to information from all over the world, and I could connect with other professionals who were facing the same challenges. It was like having a global network of colleagues at my fingertips."

CompuServe's forums were particularly influential in shaping early online communities. David Nelson, a technology enthusiast who frequented CompuServe's computer forums, remembers the sense of camaraderie that developed among users. "We were all learning together," he said. "There was a real sense of community—people were eager to help each other out, whether it was troubleshooting a problem or sharing new ideas."

Reflections from AOL Employees: AOL's rapid rise to dominance in the online services market was driven in large part by its employees, many of whom were passionate about making the internet accessible to everyone. Jane Parker, who worked in AOL's customer service department, recalls the excitement of being part of a company that was changing the world. "We knew we were part of something big," she said. "Every day, we were helping people get online for the first time, and it was incredibly rewarding to see how excited they were about it."

AOL's innovative marketing strategies were also key to its success. Mark Davidson, a former AOL marketing executive, remembers the impact of the company's free trial CDs. "The CDs were everywhere—you couldn't go to a store without seeing them," he said. "It was a brilliant strategy because it lowered the barrier to entry. People could try AOL for free, and once they were hooked, they became paying subscribers. It was a game-changer."

Experiences from Delphi Users: For early Delphi users, the service provided a gateway to the broader internet. John Simmons, an IT professional who used Delphi in the early 1990s, recalls the thrill of being able to browse the World Wide Web for the first time. "Delphi was one of the first places where you could really experience the web," he said. "I remember the first time I accessed a website—it was a simple page with some text and links, but it felt like a glimpse into the future. It was clear that this was where everything was headed."

Delphi's decision to offer internet access was a bold move that positioned it as a leader in the transition to the open internet. "They were ahead of their time," Simmons said. "By giving people access to the web, Delphi helped to demystify the internet and showed that it was something everyone could use."

The WELL: A Haven for Intellectuals and Creatives: The WELL was known for attracting a diverse group of users, including writers, artists, and technologists. Howard Rheingold, an early member of The WELL and author of "The Virtual Community," recalls the platform as a place where deep, meaningful conversations could flourish. "The WELL was different from other online services," he said. "It wasn't just about technology—it was about ideas. People came to The WELL to think, to share, and to challenge each other. It was a true community in every sense of the word."

For many users, The WELL provided a sense of belonging that was difficult to find elsewhere. "There was something special about The WELL," said Ellen Ullman, a software engineer and writer who was active on the platform. "It was a place where you could be yourself, where your ideas were taken seriously. I made lifelong friends there—people who I still talk to today."

Conclusion

The early online services like CompuServe, AOL, Delphi, and The WELL were pioneers of the digital age, laying the groundwork for the modern internet. These services introduced millions of people to the possibilities of online communication, information sharing, and community-building, long before the World Wide Web became mainstream.

CompuServe's role as a comprehensive online service, AOL's user-friendly approach and widespread adoption, Delphi's early embrace of the World Wide Web, and The WELL's unique intellectual and creative community all contributed to the development of the digital culture we know today. The personal stories from users and employees highlight the impact these services had on individuals and society, shaping the way we interact with technology and each other.

As we continue to explore the history of the internet, it's clear that these early online services were more than just technical innovations—they were cultural phenomena that changed the way we live, work, and connect. Their legacy lives on in the modern internet, where the principles of accessibility, community, and the free exchange of ideas continue to drive

TONY YUSTEIN

innovation and progress.

CHAPTER 9: THE SEARCH FOR INFORMATION: ALTA VISTA AND BEYOND

Overview

This chapter delves into the development of search engines, focusing on the pioneering role of Alta Vista and its contributions to the early web search landscape. We will explore the creation and features of Alta Vista, its impact on the evolution of web search, the competitive environment among early search engines, and the eventual rise of Google, which came to dominate the search engine market and redefine how information is accessed on the internet.

The Creation and Features of Alta Vista

The Birth of Alta Vista: Alta Vista was launched on December 15, 1995, by Digital Equipment Corporation (DEC), a major computer company at the time. It was created by a team led by Louis Monier and Michael Burrows, with the goal of showcasing the power of DEC's AlphaServer 8400 TurboLaser processor. The search engine's name, "Alta Vista," was inspired by the Spanish phrase meaning "high view," symbolizing the project's ambition to provide a comprehensive view of the rapidly expanding World Wide Web.

Alta Vista quickly became one of the most popular and influential search engines of the early internet era. At a time when the web was growing exponentially, Alta Vista offered users a powerful tool for finding information online. Its speed, reliability, and innovative features set it apart from other search engines of the time and made it a favorite among early internet users.

Key Features of Alta Vista: Alta Vista introduced several groundbreaking features that helped to shape the development of web search:

- **Comprehensive Indexing:** Alta Vista was one of the first search engines to index the full text of web pages rather than just metadata or titles. This approach allowed Alta Vista to offer more relevant and comprehensive search results, as users could search for specific phrases or keywords within the body of a webpage. By the time of its launch, Alta Vista had indexed over 20 million web pages, a staggering number for the time.

- **Boolean Search:** Alta Vista supported advanced search queries using Boolean operators such as AND, OR, and NOT. This allowed users to perform more precise searches, filtering results to match their specific needs. This feature was particularly useful for researchers and professionals who required accurate and detailed information.

- **Multilingual Search:** Recognizing the global nature of the internet, Alta Vista offered multilingual search capabilities, allowing users to search for content in different languages. This feature broadened the appeal of Alta Vista and made it a valuable tool for users around the world.

- **User-Friendly Interface:** Alta Vista's interface was clean, simple, and user-friendly. The search engine's homepage prominently featured a search box and a few options for advanced search queries, making it easy for users to quickly find what they were looking for without distractions.

Alta Vista's Popularity and Impact: Alta Vista quickly gained a large user base, becoming one of the most visited websites on the internet in the mid-to-late 1990s. Its speed and comprehensive indexing made it a favorite among both casual users and professionals. The search engine was praised for its ability to deliver relevant results quickly, which was a significant advantage in an era when internet connections were often slow and unreliable.

Alta Vista's popularity also had a broader impact on the development of the internet. It demonstrated the potential of search engines to make the vast amount of information on the web accessible and manageable. This realization spurred further innovation in the field of search technology and laid the groundwork for the development of more sophisticated search engines in the years to come.

The Role of Alta Vista in Shaping Web Search

Pioneering Full-Text Search: One of Alta Vista's most significant contributions to the field of web search was its pioneering use of full-text search. Before Alta Vista, most search engines indexed only the titles or metadata of web pages, which limited their ability to return relevant results for complex queries. By indexing the full text of web pages, Alta Vista allowed users to search for specific phrases or concepts within the content of a page, vastly improving the relevance of search results.

This approach to indexing set a new standard for search engines and influenced the design of future search technologies. The ability to search the full text of web pages made it easier for users to find the information they needed, even if it was buried deep within a lengthy document or article.

Introduction of Multimedia Search: Alta Vista was also one of the first search engines to offer multimedia search capabilities, allowing users to search for images, audio, and video files in addition to text. This feature expanded the scope of what users could discover on the web and highlighted the potential of search engines as tools for accessing a wide range of digital content.

The introduction of multimedia search was a significant step forward in the evolution of search technology. It reflected the growing diversity of content available on the internet and the need for search engines to adapt to different types of media. Alta Vista's multimedia search capabilities laid the foundation for the development of specialized search engines and features, such as Google Images and YouTube search, that would emerge in the years that followed.

Search as a Gateway to the Web: Alta Vista played a crucial role in establishing search engines as the primary gateway to the web. In the early days of the internet, navigating the web was often a daunting task, with users relying on directories and manually curated lists of websites. Alta Vista changed this by offering a more dynamic and comprehensive way to explore the web. Users could enter a query and instantly access a wealth of information, making the internet more accessible and user-friendly.

This shift in how people accessed information online had a profound impact on the development of the internet. Search engines became essential tools for navigating the web, and their importance only grew as the amount of content available online continued to expand. Alta Vista's success demonstrated the value of search engines in organizing and making sense of the vast and unstructured information on the web, setting the stage for the dominance of search as a key function of the internet.

The Competition Between Early Search Engines

The Search Engine Landscape in the 1990s: The mid-to-late 1990s were a period of intense competition and rapid innovation in the search engine market. As the internet grew in popularity, a number of search engines emerged, each offering different features and approaches to indexing and retrieving information. Some of the notable search engines that competed with Alta Vista during this period included:

- **Yahoo!:** Originally launched as a web directory, Yahoo! quickly became one of the most popular destinations on the web. Although it started as a manually curated directory of websites, Yahoo! eventually integrated search capabilities powered by other search engines, including Alta Vista and later Inktomi. Yahoo!'s combination of a directory and search engine made it a powerful tool for navigating the web.
- **Lycos:** Founded in 1994 by Michael Loren Mauldin, Lycos was one of the earliest search engines to offer full-text search capabilities, similar to Alta Vista. Lycos differentiated itself by offering a broader range of services, including web hosting and email, in addition to search. Lycos gained a significant following and became one of the most visited sites on the web during the late 1990s.
- **Excite:** Launched in 1995, Excite offered a search engine that combined full-text search with a curated directory of websites. Excite also introduced personalized features, such as customizable homepages and email, which helped it attract a loyal user base. Like Lycos, Excite expanded its offerings to include a wide range of online services.
- **Infoseek:** Infoseek was another major player in the early search engine market, known for its fast and accurate search results. Founded in 1994, Infoseek focused on providing a simple and efficient search experience. It was one of the first search engines to offer sponsored search results, paving the way for the

development of the search advertising industry.

The Battle for Market Share: The competition between these early search engines was fierce, with each company vying to become the dominant player in the rapidly expanding online search market. This competition drove innovation, as search engines continually sought to improve their indexing algorithms, search speed, and user interfaces. The introduction of new features, such as personalized search, multimedia search, and customizable homepages, reflected the evolving needs and preferences of internet users.

Despite Alta Vista's early success and technical superiority, it faced challenges from its competitors, who offered unique features and services that attracted users. For example, Yahoo!'s integration of search with a comprehensive web directory made it a popular choice for users who preferred a more curated approach to web navigation. Meanwhile, Lycos and Excite attracted users with their all-in-one portal services, which combined search with email, news, and entertainment.

Strategic Partnerships and Acquisitions: As the competition intensified, many search engines sought strategic partnerships and acquisitions to strengthen their positions in the market. For example, Yahoo! acquired the search engine Inktomi in 2002, while Lycos was acquired by Terra Networks, a subsidiary of the Spanish telecommunications company Telefónica, in 2000. These moves were part of a broader trend of consolidation in the search engine market, as companies sought to build integrated platforms that could compete with emerging giants like Google.

Despite these efforts, many of the early search engines struggled to maintain their market share in the face of increasing competition and the rapid pace of technological change. As the search landscape evolved, it became clear that the future of search would be dominated by a new generation of search engines, led by a company that would revolutionize the industry.

The Eventual Rise of Google and Its Dominance in Search

The Founding of Google: Google was founded in 1998 by Larry Page and Sergey Brin, two Ph.D. students at Stanford University. Their goal was to create a search engine that could deliver more relevant search results by analyzing the relationships between websites, rather than just matching keywords. This approach, known as PageRank, ranked webpages based on the number and quality of links pointing to them, with the idea that more important pages would have more links from other pages. Page and Brin initially named their search engine "Backrub," reflecting its focus on analyzing backlinks, but soon changed the name to "Google," a play on the mathematical term "googol," representing the vast amounts of information the search engine was designed to handle.

Google's PageRank algorithm was a significant innovation that set it apart from other search engines. By prioritizing search results based on the web's natural link structure, Google was able to deliver more relevant and accurate results than its competitors. This focus on relevance quickly resonated with users, who found that Google consistently provided better answers to their queries than other search engines.

Google's Rise to Dominance: Google's rise to dominance in the search engine market was rapid and driven by several key factors:

1. **Superior Search Results:** Google's use of the PageRank algorithm, combined with a clean and simple interface, allowed it to deliver highly relevant search results quickly. Users appreciated the efficiency and accuracy of Google's search engine, which often outperformed established competitors like Alta Vista, Yahoo!, and Lycos.

2. **Minimalist Interface:** While other search engines of the time were evolving into portals filled with ads, news, and various services, Google maintained

a minimalist approach. Its homepage featured little more than a search box and a "Google Search" button, which appealed to users who wanted a fast, no-frills search experience.

3. **Strategic Partnerships and Expansion:** Google's growth was further accelerated by strategic partnerships. In 2000, Google became the default search engine for Yahoo!, which had previously relied on its own search technology. This partnership significantly increased Google's visibility and user base, helping to establish it as a leading search engine.

4. **AdWords and Monetization:** In 2000, Google launched AdWords, a revolutionary advertising platform that allowed businesses to bid on keywords to have their ads appear alongside search results. AdWords was based on a pay-per-click (PPC) model, where advertisers paid only when users clicked on their ads. This innovation provided Google with a lucrative revenue stream and helped it maintain its focus on delivering high-quality search results without cluttering its interface with banner ads and pop-ups.

5. **Innovation and Continuous Improvement:** Google's commitment to innovation and continuous improvement kept it ahead of the competition. The company constantly refined its search algorithms, improved its indexing capabilities, and introduced new features, such as Google Images (launched in 2001) and Google News (launched in 2002). These innovations not only enhanced the search experience but also expanded Google's reach into new areas of information retrieval.

Impact on the Search Engine Market: As Google's popularity grew, it began to dominate the search engine market, displacing many of its early competitors. By the mid-2000s, Google had become the most widely used search engine in the world, with a market share that dwarfed that of its rivals. This dominance was further cemented by Google's continued investment in its infrastructure, which allowed it to index and search more of the web than any other search engine.

The success of Google also had a profound impact on the broader internet ecosystem. As search became the primary way that users navigated the web, the importance of appearing in Google's search results grew, leading to the rise of search engine optimization (SEO) as a key aspect of online marketing. Google's influence extended beyond search, as the company expanded into areas such as online advertising, cloud computing, and mobile technology, shaping the future of the internet in the process.

Challenges and Criticisms: Despite its success, Google has faced challenges and criticisms over the years. Concerns about privacy, data collection, and the company's dominance in the search and advertising markets have led to regulatory scrutiny and legal challenges in various countries. Critics have also raised concerns about the potential for bias in Google's search algorithms, which could influence what information users see.

Nevertheless, Google's impact on the search engine market and the internet as a whole is undeniable. The company's ability to innovate and adapt has allowed it to maintain its position as the world's leading search engine, even as the internet landscape has evolved.

Conclusion

The evolution of search engines from the early days of Alta Vista to the dominance of Google has been a transformative journey that has reshaped how we access and interact with information. Alta Vista's pioneering contributions, such as full-text search and multimedia capabilities, set the stage for the development of more sophisticated search technologies. The competition between early search engines drove innovation and pushed the boundaries of what was possible in information retrieval.

Google's rise to dominance, fueled by its innovative PageRank algorithm, minimalist interface, and strategic monetization through AdWords, revolutionized the search engine market and established new standards for relevance and user experience. As the gateway to the web, Google has become an integral part of daily life for billions of people, shaping the way we find and use information.

The story of search engines is one of continuous innovation and adaptation, as new technologies and challenges have emerged over time. As we continue to explore the history of the internet, it is clear that search engines have played a central role in making the vast amounts of information on the web accessible and useful, driving the digital revolution and connecting people to the knowledge and resources they need.

CHAPTER 10: FIDONET: THE GLOBAL BBS NETWORK

Overview

This chapter provides an in-depth exploration of FidoNet, the largest and most influential Bulletin Board System (BBS) network of its time. We will examine the origins and expansion of FidoNet, how it connected BBSs worldwide, the challenges and successes of managing a decentralized network, and FidoNet's lasting legacy in the history of online communication.

The Origins and Expansion of FidoNet

The Birth of FidoNet: FidoNet was created in 1984 by Tom Jennings, a software engineer and BBS operator in San Francisco. At the time, Jennings was running a small BBS called Fido BBS, named after his dog. Jennings was frustrated by the limitations of the existing BBS software, which made it difficult for operators to exchange messages and files with other BBSs. To solve this problem, he developed a system that allowed BBSs to connect and exchange information automatically, without requiring human intervention.

This system became known as FidoNet, and it was revolutionary in its ability to link together geographically dispersed BBSs into a single, cohesive network. FidoNet used a store-and-forward messaging system, where messages were bundled together and transmitted between BBSs during off-peak hours, typically late at night, to minimize long-distance telephone charges. This approach allowed BBS operators to connect their systems into a global network without incurring significant costs.

The Growth of FidoNet: FidoNet grew rapidly as more BBS operators adopted Jennings' software. The network's open architecture and ease of use made it an attractive option for BBS operators around the world who wanted to connect their systems to a broader community. By the mid-1980s, FidoNet had expanded to include thousands of BBSs in dozens of countries, making it the largest BBS network in existence.

The growth of FidoNet was driven by the enthusiasm of its users and operators, who saw the network as a way to democratize online communication. Unlike the proprietary online services of the time, which were often expensive and closed off to all but the most dedicated users, FidoNet was free and open to anyone with access to a BBS. This openness fostered a sense of community among FidoNet users and contributed to the network's rapid expansion.

FidoNet's Role in Global Communication: FidoNet played a crucial role in enabling global communication during a time when the internet was still in its infancy. Through FidoNet, users could send messages (known as "Netmail") to other users anywhere in the world, participate in public discussions on a wide range of topics (known as "echomail"), and share files and software with others in the network. This level of connectivity was unprecedented for many users, who were now able to communicate with people from different countries and cultures without leaving their homes.

FidoNet also provided a platform for grassroots activism and the free exchange of information, particularly in countries where access to information was restricted. For example, during the late 1980s and early 1990s, FidoNet was used by activists in Eastern Europe to share news and information that was censored by their governments. The network's decentralized structure made it difficult for authorities to control or shut down, making it a valuable tool for those seeking to bypass state censorship.

How FidoNet Connected BBSs Worldwide

The Store-and-Forward Model: FidoNet's key innovation was its store-and-forward model of communication. In this system, messages and files were stored on a BBS and then forwarded to other BBSs during scheduled "mail runs." These mail runs typically occurred during off-peak hours, when telephone rates were lower, to reduce the cost of long-distance communication.

The process worked as follows:

1. **Message Creation:** A user would create a message or upload a file to their local BBS.
2. **Bundling:** The BBS would bundle the messages and files into a "packet," which contained all the data that needed to be sent to other BBSs.
3. **Routing:** The BBS would determine the best route for the packet to take, based on a hierarchical network of "zones," "regions," and "nodes" that made up FidoNet.
4. **Transmission:** During the next scheduled mail run, the BBS would initiate a connection to the next BBS in the packet's route and transmit the packet. This process would continue until the packet reached its destination BBS.
5. **Delivery:** The destination BBS would unbundle the packet and deliver the messages and files to the intended recipients.

This system allowed FidoNet to operate efficiently and cost-effectively, even though it relied on the public telephone network rather than dedicated lines. The use of store-and-forward communication also meant that FidoNet could scale easily as more BBSs joined the network, making it possible for the network to expand globally.

The FidoNet Nodelist: A critical component of FidoNet was the Nodelist, a directory of all the BBSs that were part of the network. The Nodelist included information such as the BBS's phone number, location, and operating hours, as well as its unique FidoNet address (a combination of zone, region, and node numbers). The Nodelist was updated regularly and distributed to all BBSs in the network, ensuring that each BBS knew how to reach every other BBS in FidoNet.

The Nodelist was more than just a directory—it was the backbone of FidoNet's routing system. The hierarchical structure of the Nodelist allowed FidoNet to route messages efficiently, even across long distances. For example, a message sent from a BBS in the United States to a BBS in Europe might pass through several intermediate BBSs (known as "hubs" or "gateways") before reaching its final destination. This hierarchical routing ensured that messages were delivered as quickly and cheaply as possible.

Connecting the World: FidoNet's ability to connect BBSs worldwide was a major breakthrough in online communication. Before FidoNet, most BBSs were isolated from one another, with users limited to communicating only with others who dialed into the same BBS. FidoNet broke down these barriers, allowing users to communicate with people from different countries, cultures, and backgrounds.

This global connectivity had a profound impact on the way people used BBSs. Users could participate in echomail discussions on topics ranging from technology and science to politics and entertainment, sharing ideas and experiences with others from around the world. FidoNet also facilitated the exchange of files and software, allowing users to access a wider range of resources than ever before.

FidoNet's global reach was particularly important in regions where access to information was restricted or limited. In

Eastern Europe, for example, FidoNet provided a lifeline for activists and dissidents who used the network to bypass government censorship and share uncensored news and information. In other parts of the world, FidoNet helped to bridge the digital divide, connecting users in developing countries with the global online community.

The Challenges and Successes of Managing a Decentralized Network

Decentralization as a Strength and Challenge: One of FidoNet's defining features was its decentralized structure. Unlike proprietary online services, which were controlled by a single company or organization, FidoNet was a grassroots network, maintained and operated by a community of volunteers. This decentralization was both a strength and a challenge for the network.

On the one hand, decentralization made FidoNet resilient and adaptable. Because the network had no central point of control, it was difficult for any single entity to shut it down or interfere with its operations. This resilience was especially important in regions where governments sought to control access to information. FidoNet's decentralized nature also allowed it to scale organically, as new BBSs could join the network without needing approval from a central authority.

On the other hand, managing a decentralized network presented significant challenges. Coordinating the activities of thousands of independent BBS operators, each with their own priorities and resources, required a high degree of cooperation and communication. Ensuring that the Nodelist was accurate and up-to-date was a constant challenge, as was maintaining the network's routing system as new BBSs joined and others left.

The Role of Coordinators: To address these challenges, FidoNet relied on a system of coordinators, who were responsible for managing different parts of the network. Coordinators were volunteers elected by their peers to oversee the activities of BBSs in their region or zone. They played a crucial role in maintaining the integrity of the network, resolving disputes, and ensuring that the Nodelist and routing system were properly maintained.

Coordinators also served as a point of contact between the different levels of the network. They communicated regularly with other coordinators and with the FidoNet International Coordinator, who was responsible for overseeing the entire network. This system of coordination helped to ensure that FidoNet operated smoothly, despite its decentralized nature.

Technical and Logistical Challenges: FidoNet faced a number of technical and logistical challenges as it expanded. One of the biggest challenges was dealing with the limitations of the public telephone network. Long-distance communication was expensive, and many BBS operators had to find creative ways to minimize costs. This often involved setting up "mail hubs" in strategic locations, where messages could be forwarded over shorter, less expensive routes.

Another challenge was the variability of BBS hardware and software. Because FidoNet was an open network, BBS operators used a wide variety of systems, each with its own capabilities and limitations. Ensuring that these systems could communicate effectively with one another required constant updates to the FidoNet software and protocols.

Despite these challenges, FidoNet succeeded in creating a **robust and expansive network** that connected thousands of BBSs around the world. The ingenuity and dedication of the FidoNet community were key to overcoming these challenges, allowing the network to thrive even in the face of technical limitations and the complexities of managing a decentralized system.

Successes and Milestones: FidoNet's successes were numerous and impactful. It became a model for decentralized networking, demonstrating how a global communication network could be built and maintained by a grassroots community of users. Some of the key milestones in FidoNet's history include:

1. **Global Reach:** By the late 1980s, FidoNet had grown to

include over 10,000 BBSs in more than 50 countries, making it the largest BBS network in the world. This global reach enabled users to communicate and share information across borders, fostering a sense of international community.

2. **Technical Innovations:** The development of FidoNet required significant technical innovation, particularly in the areas of network routing and message handling. The FidoNet protocol became a de facto standard for BBS communication, influencing the design of other networking systems that followed.

3. **Cultural Impact:** FidoNet played a crucial role in shaping the culture of early online communication. The network's open and democratic structure encouraged participation and collaboration, and its emphasis on free speech and the exchange of ideas made it a haven for those seeking to communicate without censorship.

4. **Political and Social Influence:** FidoNet's role in political and social movements, particularly in regions with restricted access to information, highlighted the power of decentralized networks to support activism and social change. The network's ability to bypass traditional communication channels made it a valuable tool for dissidents, activists, and independent journalists.

FidoNet's Legacy in the History of Online Communication

Influence on the Internet: FidoNet's legacy is deeply intertwined with the development of the modern internet. Many of the concepts and technologies pioneered by FidoNet, such as decentralized communication, message routing, and the use of networks to connect disparate communities, were later incorporated into the design of the internet.

The success of FidoNet demonstrated the viability of large-scale, decentralized networks, providing a blueprint for how such systems could be managed and scaled. The lessons learned from FidoNet informed the development of internet protocols and networking practices, particularly in the early days of the internet when many of the foundational technologies were still being established.

Community and Collaboration: One of FidoNet's most enduring legacies is its emphasis on community and collaboration. The network was built and maintained by volunteers who were passionate about using technology to connect people and share information. This spirit of collaboration and the commitment to open communication helped to establish the norms and values that continue to shape online communities today.

FidoNet also fostered a sense of ownership and responsibility among its users. Because the network was decentralized and operated by its members, users had a direct stake in its success and were actively involved in maintaining and improving the system. This sense of community and shared responsibility is a key element of many modern online platforms and communities.

The Transition to the Internet: As the internet grew in popularity during the 1990s, many BBSs, including those on FidoNet, began to transition to internet-based services. The rise of the World Wide Web, email, and internet forums offered new opportunities for communication and information sharing, leading to a gradual decline in the use of BBS networks like FidoNet.

However, the transition from FidoNet to the internet was not a sudden or complete abandonment of the BBS model. Many BBS operators and users embraced the internet as a new way to connect with others, and FidoNet's principles of decentralized communication and community-driven networks found new life in the emerging digital landscape. In many ways, FidoNet served as a bridge between the pre-internet era of online communication and the modern internet, helping to shape the culture and infrastructure of the digital age.

Continued Relevance: Although FidoNet's influence has waned since its heyday, the network still exists today, maintained by a small but dedicated group of enthusiasts. For these users, FidoNet represents a piece of internet history and a reminder of the early days of online communication. The network continues to operate, connecting BBSs around the world and preserving the legacy of a time when the internet was still in its infancy.

FidoNet's continued existence is a testament to the enduring appeal of decentralized networks and the importance of community in online communication. While the internet has evolved in ways that far surpass the capabilities of FidoNet, the principles that underpinned the network—openness, collaboration, and resilience—remain as relevant as ever.

Conclusion

FidoNet was a pioneering network that played a crucial role in the development of online communication. By connecting BBSs around the world, FidoNet created a global community of users who could share information, collaborate on projects, and engage in discussions on a wide range of topics. The network's decentralized structure and innovative use of store-and-forward communication allowed it to scale rapidly, becoming the largest BBS network in the world.

FidoNet's legacy is evident in the way it influenced the development of the internet and the culture of online communication. The network's emphasis on community, collaboration, and free speech helped to establish the norms and values that continue to shape the digital world today. While FidoNet's prominence has diminished over time, its impact on the history of online communication remains significant.

As we continue to explore the evolution of the internet, it is important to recognize the role that networks like FidoNet played in laying the foundation for the connected world we live in today. The story of FidoNet is a reminder of the power of technology to bring people together and the importance of maintaining an open and inclusive approach to online communication.

CHAPTER 11: THE WORLD WIDE WEB: A NEW DIMENSION

Overview

This chapter explores the invention of the World Wide Web by Tim Berners-Lee, its transformative impact on internet usage, and its rapid adoption across the globe. We will examine the development of the first web browser and server, the role of early web browsers like Mosaic and Netscape Navigator, and the explosion of websites that followed. Additionally, we will discuss the creation of web standards that helped shape the web into the dynamic and universally accessible platform it is today.

The Development of the First Web Browser and Server

The Birth of the World Wide Web: The World Wide Web was invented by Tim Berners-Lee, a British computer scientist working at CERN (the European Organization for Nuclear Research) in Geneva, Switzerland. In 1989, Berners-Lee proposed a system that would allow researchers at CERN to easily share documents and data across different computers and networks. This system, which he initially called "Mesh," was later renamed the World Wide Web.

Berners-Lee's vision for the World Wide Web was to create a decentralized, hypertext-based system that would allow users to navigate between documents linked together by "hyperlinks."

This concept was inspired by earlier work on hypertext systems, such as Ted Nelson's Project Xanadu, but Berners-Lee extended these ideas by combining hypertext with the emerging internet infrastructure.

The First Web Browser and Server: In 1990, Berners-Lee developed the first web browser, known as "WorldWideWeb" (later renamed "Nexus"), and the first web server, called "httpd" (short for HyperText Transfer Protocol Daemon). The WorldWideWeb browser was a graphical user interface (GUI) application that allowed users to view and navigate web pages using hyperlinks. It also had editing capabilities, enabling users to create and modify web content directly within the browser.

The first web server, running on a NeXT computer at CERN, hosted the world's first website, which provided information about the World Wide Web project and instructions on how to set up a web server and create web pages. This website, which is still accessible today, is often referred to as the "mother of all websites."

The Core Technologies: Berners-Lee's invention of the World Wide Web was built on three core technologies:

1. **HTML (HyperText Markup Language):** HTML is the standard language used to create web pages. It allows users to structure text, images, and other content using a system of tags and attributes. HTML is the foundation of web content and remains the primary language for creating web pages.

2. **HTTP (HyperText Transfer Protocol):** HTTP is the protocol used to transmit data between web servers and web browsers. It defines how requests and responses are formatted and exchanged over the internet. HTTP is the backbone of web communication, enabling the seamless exchange of information across the web.

3. **URI (Uniform Resource Identifier):** A URI is a string of characters used to identify a resource on the web, such as a webpage, image, or document. The most common type of URI is the URL (Uniform Resource Locator), which specifies the location of a resource and how to access it. URIs are essential for linking and navigating the web.

These technologies, combined with Berners-Lee's vision of a decentralized and open web, laid the groundwork for the rapid expansion and adoption of the World Wide Web.

How the World Wide Web Transformed Internet Usage

From Niche to Mainstream: Before the advent of the World Wide Web, the internet was primarily used by researchers, academics, and government institutions for tasks such as email, file transfer, and remote access to computer systems. The introduction of the World Wide Web transformed the internet from a specialized tool into a global information network accessible to anyone with a computer and a modem.

The World Wide Web made it possible for users to navigate the vast and growing amounts of information on the internet using simple point-and-click interfaces. The use of hypertext allowed for non-linear navigation, enabling users to explore related topics and resources with ease. This new way of interacting with information was intuitive and user-friendly, making the internet more accessible to the general public.

The Democratization of Information: The World Wide Web democratized access to information by allowing anyone to create and publish content online. This was a significant departure from the traditional media landscape, where information was controlled by a few large organizations. With the web, individuals, small businesses, and non-profit organizations could reach a global audience without the need for expensive infrastructure or distribution channels.

The rapid expansion of web content in the 1990s reflected this democratization. Websites dedicated to a wide range of topics, from hobbies and interests to news and politics, began to appear. This explosion of content made the web an invaluable resource for information, education, and entertainment, and it contributed to the growth of the internet as a cultural and economic force.

The Rise of E-Commerce and Online Services: The World Wide Web also paved the way for the rise of e-commerce and online services. Companies quickly recognized the potential of the web as a platform for reaching customers and conducting business. The ability to create interactive and visually appealing websites allowed businesses to showcase their products and services, while the development of secure online payment systems enabled the growth of online shopping.

One of the earliest and most successful examples of e-commerce was Amazon.com, which was founded by Jeff Bezos in 1994 as an online bookstore. Amazon quickly expanded its offerings to include a wide range of products, becoming a major player in the retail industry. Similarly, eBay, founded in 1995, revolutionized online auctions and peer-to-peer sales.

The World Wide Web also facilitated the growth of online services such as email, news, and entertainment. Websites like Yahoo! and MSN offered users a one-stop portal for accessing a variety of services, including search, email, news, and weather. These portals became popular entry points to the web, helping to drive further adoption of internet services.

The Impact on Communication and Social Interaction: The World Wide Web fundamentally changed the way people communicate and interact with one another. Email and online messaging became more widely used as the web made it easier to connect with others, regardless of geographic location. The introduction of web-based forums and chat rooms provided new platforms for social interaction and community building.

The web also enabled the rise of social media, which would become one of the most significant developments in online communication. Early social networking sites like SixDegrees.com, launched in 1997, and Friendster, launched in 2002, allowed users to create profiles, connect with friends, and share content. These platforms laid the groundwork for the social media giants that would emerge in the 2000s, such as Facebook and Twitter.

The Role of Early Web Browsers Like Mosaic and Netscape Navigator

Mosaic: The First Popular Web Browser: Mosaic, developed in 1993 by Marc Andreessen and Eric Bina at the National Center for Supercomputing Applications (NCSA) at the University of Illinois, was the first web browser to gain widespread popularity. Mosaic was notable for its graphical interface, which allowed users to view images inline with text on web pages. This visual appeal, combined with its ease of use, made Mosaic a breakthrough in the adoption of the World Wide Web.

Mosaic's impact on the web was profound. It introduced many people to the World Wide Web for the first time and set the standard for future web browsers. The success of Mosaic helped to drive the rapid growth of the web, as more users and developers began creating and exploring web content.

Netscape Navigator: The Birth of the Commercial Browser: Netscape Navigator, launched in 1994 by Netscape Communications Corporation (founded by Marc Andreessen and Jim Clark), was the first commercially successful web browser. Built on the foundation of Mosaic, Netscape Navigator introduced several key innovations that improved the web browsing experience, including faster page loading, support for multimedia content, and enhanced security features.

Netscape Navigator quickly became the dominant web browser, capturing over 90% of the market by the mid-1990s. Its success was driven by its user-friendly interface, robust performance, and the fact that it was available for free to non-commercial users. Netscape's dominance in the browser market also helped to accelerate the development of the World Wide Web, as more users and businesses adopted the platform.

The Browser Wars: The success of Netscape Navigator set the stage for the "browser wars" of the late 1990s, a period of intense competition between Netscape and Microsoft's Internet Explorer. Microsoft, recognizing the strategic importance of web browsers, released Internet Explorer in 1995 as part of the Windows 95 Plus! Pack. Over the next few years, Microsoft invested heavily in improving Internet Explorer, integrating it with the Windows operating system, and aggressively marketing it to consumers.

The browser wars were characterized by rapid innovation and the introduction of new features, as both companies sought to gain a competitive edge. This competition drove the development of web standards, as both Netscape and Microsoft introduced proprietary technologies that were not always compatible with one another. The resulting fragmentation of the web led to the creation of the World Wide Web Consortium (W3C), which was established in 1994 to develop and promote open web standards that would ensure interoperability across different browsers and platforms.

The Legacy of Early Web Browsers: The early web browsers like Mosaic and Netscape Navigator played a crucial role in popularizing the World Wide Web and shaping the future of internet usage. They introduced millions of users to the web, provided a platform for the growth of web content, and established the importance of user-friendly interfaces in technology adoption.

The legacy of these early browsers can be seen in the modern web, where browsers continue to be the primary gateway to online content and services. The innovations introduced by Mosaic and Netscape, such **as graphical interfaces, inline images, and support for multimedia content,** laid the foundation for the modern web browsing experience. These early browsers set standards that have persisted and evolved, influencing the design of contemporary browsers like Google Chrome, Mozilla Firefox, and Apple's Safari.

Netscape's role in the browser wars also underscored the significance of web browsers as a key battleground for control over the internet. The competition between Netscape Navigator and Internet Explorer not only drove rapid technological advancement but also highlighted the importance of open standards and the dangers of monopolistic practices in the software industry.

The Fall of Netscape and the Rise of Internet Explorer: Despite its early dominance, Netscape Navigator eventually lost its market share to Internet Explorer. Microsoft's aggressive bundling of Internet Explorer with the Windows operating system, combined with substantial investments in improving the browser's performance and features, allowed Internet Explorer to overtake Netscape by the late 1990s.

The decline of Netscape was marked by its acquisition by AOL in 1998. While AOL initially hoped to use Netscape to challenge Microsoft's dominance, the browser's market share continued to decline as Internet Explorer became the de facto standard for web browsing. By the early 2000s, Netscape Navigator had largely disappeared from the market.

However, the legacy of Netscape lived on in the form of the Mozilla project, which was launched by Netscape in 1998 as an open-source initiative to develop a new web browser based on the Netscape codebase. This project eventually led to the creation of Mozilla Firefox, a browser that remains popular to this day and continues to champion the principles of open standards and user choice in the web ecosystem.

The Explosion of Websites and the Creation of Web Standards

The Rapid Growth of Web Content: The launch of early web browsers like Mosaic and Netscape Navigator coincided with an explosion of web content. As more people gained access to the

World Wide Web, the number of websites grew exponentially. In 1993, there were only around 130 websites; by 1996, this number had skyrocketed to over 100,000.

This rapid growth was fueled by the web's open nature, which allowed anyone with basic technical skills to create and publish a website. The early web was a diverse and eclectic space, filled with personal homepages, fan sites, academic resources, and the first commercial websites. The web became a platform for creativity and self-expression, as well as a powerful tool for business and communication.

The Development of Web Standards: As the web grew, the need for standardized protocols and technologies became increasingly apparent. In the early days of the web, different browsers often implemented proprietary features and tags, leading to compatibility issues and a fragmented user experience. To address these challenges, the World Wide Web Consortium (W3C) was established in 1994 by Tim Berners-Lee.

The W3C's mission was to develop and promote open web standards that would ensure the long-term growth and interoperability of the World Wide Web. Some of the key standards developed by the W3C include:

- **HTML (HyperText Markup Language):** HTML continued to evolve under the guidance of the W3C, with new versions adding support for multimedia elements, forms, and more complex layouts. HTML 4.0, released in 1997, introduced support for stylesheets and scripting, paving the way for more dynamic and visually appealing websites.
- **CSS (Cascading Style Sheets):** CSS was introduced by the W3C in 1996 as a way to separate the presentation of a webpage from its content. CSS allowed web designers to control the layout, fonts, colors, and other visual aspects of a website using a separate stylesheet, making it easier to maintain and update websites.

- **XML (eXtensible Markup Language):** XML, introduced in 1998, was a flexible markup language that allowed developers to create custom tags and data structures. XML played a crucial role in the development of web services and the exchange of data between different systems.
- **JavaScript:** While not directly developed by the W3C, JavaScript became an essential component of the modern web. Introduced by Netscape in 1995, JavaScript allowed developers to create interactive and dynamic web pages. The W3C later worked to standardize JavaScript through the ECMAScript specification.

These and other standards helped to create a more consistent and accessible web experience for users, while also enabling developers to build more complex and sophisticated websites.

The Impact of Web Standards on the Web's Evolution: The adoption of web standards was instrumental in the evolution of the World Wide Web. By providing a common framework for web development, standards like HTML, CSS, and JavaScript enabled the creation of websites that were compatible across different browsers and devices. This interoperability was crucial for the web's expansion into new markets and the proliferation of new devices, including smartphones and tablets.

Web standards also played a key role in ensuring the accessibility of the web. The W3C developed guidelines for creating websites that were accessible to people with disabilities, including those with visual impairments. These guidelines, known as the Web Content Accessibility Guidelines (WCAG), have been widely adopted and continue to shape the design of accessible websites.

The creation of web standards was not without challenges. The "browser wars" of the late 1990s and early 2000s saw major browser vendors, particularly Microsoft and Netscape, competing to introduce new features and technologies that were not always compatible with existing standards. This led to a period of fragmentation, where websites often had to be tailored for specific browsers, undermining the promise of a universal web.

Despite these challenges, the W3C's commitment to open standards helped to guide the web through this period of rapid growth and change. By the early 2000s, web standards had become widely accepted, and the web was on its way to becoming the interoperable and accessible platform envisioned by its creators.

Conclusion

The invention of the World Wide Web by Tim Berners-Lee was a transformative moment in the history of the internet. The development of the first web browser and server, along with the core technologies of HTML, HTTP, and URI, laid the foundation for a global information network that would revolutionize communication, commerce, and culture.

The rapid adoption of the World Wide Web, driven by the introduction of user-friendly web browsers like Mosaic and Netscape Navigator, marked the beginning of a new era in internet usage. The web democratized access to information, empowered individuals and businesses to create and share content, and fundamentally changed the way people interacted with the world.

The explosion of websites that followed the web's launch reflected the immense creative and entrepreneurial energy unleashed by this new medium. The development of web standards by the W3C ensured that the web remained open, accessible, and interoperable, enabling its continued growth and evolution.

As we look back on the early days of the World Wide Web, it is clear that this innovation has had a profound and lasting impact on the world. The web has become an essential part of modern life, connecting billions of people and serving as a platform for communication, learning, and innovation. The legacy of the World Wide Web continues to shape the future of the internet, as new technologies and applications build on the foundation laid by Tim Berners-Lee and the early pioneers of the web.

CHAPTER 12: THE IMPACT OF WINDOWS 95 AND INTERNET EXPLORER

Overview

This chapter explores the profound influence of Windows 95 and Internet Explorer on the internet landscape, delving into the strategic bundling of Internet Explorer with Windows 95, the ensuing browser wars between Internet Explorer and Netscape, the antitrust cases brought against Microsoft, and the lasting impact of Windows 95 on personal computing and internet access.

The Bundling of Internet Explorer with Windows 95

Strategic Integration: The release of Windows 95 in August 1995 marked a significant milestone in the history of personal computing. One of the most impactful decisions Microsoft made during the development of Windows 95 was to bundle its web browser, Internet Explorer (IE), with the operating system. This integration was a strategic move by Microsoft to leverage the dominance of its Windows operating system to promote Internet Explorer as the default web browser for millions of users.

At the time, the World Wide Web was rapidly growing in

popularity, and web browsers were becoming an essential tool for accessing the internet. By including Internet Explorer as part of the Windows 95 package, Microsoft ensured that users had immediate access to a web browser upon installing the operating system. This was a significant advantage, especially for less tech-savvy users who might not have been inclined to seek out and install a third-party browser.

The Impact on Browser Adoption: The bundling of Internet Explorer with Windows 95 had a profound impact on browser adoption. Prior to the release of Windows 95, Netscape Navigator was the dominant web browser, with a significant market share. However, the inclusion of Internet Explorer in Windows 95 allowed Microsoft to quickly capture a large portion of the browser market.

For many users, the convenience of having a pre-installed browser meant that Internet Explorer became their default choice for web browsing. As a result, Internet Explorer's market share began to grow rapidly, posing a serious threat to Netscape's dominance. This shift in market dynamics set the stage for the "browser wars," a period of intense competition between Microsoft and Netscape.

Microsoft's Aggressive Tactics: Microsoft did not stop at simply bundling Internet Explorer with Windows 95; the company also engaged in aggressive tactics to promote its browser and undermine its competitors. For instance, Microsoft entered into exclusive agreements with PC manufacturers, requiring them to pre-install Internet Explorer on their machines and, in some cases, prohibiting them from pre-installing Netscape Navigator.

Additionally, Microsoft tied Internet Explorer more deeply into the Windows operating system, making it difficult for users to remove or disable the browser. This integration further discouraged users from installing alternative browsers, as Internet Explorer was seamlessly integrated with the Windows desktop environment, file manager, and other system components.

These tactics, while effective in boosting Internet Explorer's market share, would later become the focus of significant legal scrutiny and contribute to the antitrust cases brought against Microsoft.

The Subsequent Browser Wars Between Internet Explorer and Netscape

The Rise of Netscape Navigator: Before the launch of Internet Explorer, Netscape Navigator was the leading web browser, commanding over 80% of the market by the mid-1990s. Netscape's early success was driven by its innovative features, ease of use, and the fact that it was one of the first browsers to support multiple platforms, including Windows, Macintosh, and Unix.

Netscape Navigator was developed by Netscape Communications Corporation, a company founded by Marc Andreessen and Jim Clark. The browser quickly became the standard for web browsing, and Netscape's initial public offering (IPO) in 1995 was one of the most successful in Silicon Valley history, signaling the dawn of the internet age.

The Intensification of the Browser Wars: The browser wars began in earnest after the release of Internet Explorer 3.0 in 1996. This version of Internet Explorer represented a significant improvement over its predecessors, with better performance, support for new web technologies, and a more polished user interface. Microsoft's aggressive distribution of Internet Explorer through Windows 95, combined with the improvements in the browser itself, allowed it to rapidly gain market share.

The competition between Netscape and Microsoft became fierce, with both companies releasing frequent updates to their browsers, adding new features, and improving performance. This period of rapid innovation benefited users, as browsers became more capable and user-friendly. However, it also led to significant fragmentation of web standards, as both companies introduced proprietary features that were not always compatible with each other.

Netscape responded to Microsoft's challenge by making its browser available for free in 1998, moving away from its original business model, which relied on selling licenses to users and corporations. Despite this move, Netscape struggled to maintain its market position as Microsoft continued to dominate the desktop environment with Windows 95 and later Windows 98, which also included Internet Explorer by default.

The Decline of Netscape: By the late 1990s, Internet Explorer had overtaken Netscape Navigator as the most widely used web browser. Netscape's market share declined rapidly as Microsoft continued to improve Internet Explorer and leverage its Windows monopoly to promote the browser. The release of Internet Explorer 4.0 in 1997 and Internet Explorer 5.0 in 1999 further solidified Microsoft's dominance, with these versions offering enhanced functionality, better support for web standards, and tighter integration with Windows.

Netscape attempted to counter Microsoft's dominance by embracing open-source development with the launch of the Mozilla project in 1998. The Mozilla project aimed to create a new, open-source browser based on the Netscape codebase. However, by this time, Netscape had already lost much of its market share, and the company was acquired by AOL in 1998. Although the Mozilla project eventually led to the creation of the Firefox browser, which remains popular today, Netscape Navigator itself continued to decline and was officially discontinued in 2008.

The Antitrust Cases Against Microsoft and Their Outcomes

The U.S. Department of Justice Antitrust Case: Microsoft's aggressive tactics during the browser wars, particularly the bundling of Internet Explorer with Windows and the company's efforts to undermine Netscape, attracted the attention of antitrust regulators. In 1998, the U.S. Department of Justice

(DOJ), along with 20 state attorneys general, filed an antitrust lawsuit against Microsoft, alleging that the company had engaged in anti-competitive practices to maintain its monopoly in the operating system market and to dominate the web browser market.

The case, often referred to as United States v. Microsoft Corp., became one of the most high-profile antitrust trials in history. The government argued that Microsoft had used its dominance in the PC operating system market to stifle competition, limit consumer choice, and maintain its monopoly. Specifically, the DOJ claimed that Microsoft's bundling of Internet Explorer with Windows was an illegal attempt to eliminate Netscape as a competitor.

The Trial and Initial Ruling: The trial began in 1998 and featured testimony from numerous witnesses, including top executives from Microsoft, Netscape, and other technology companies. The government presented evidence that Microsoft had engaged in a range of anti-competitive behaviors, including exclusive deals with PC manufacturers, efforts to block the distribution of Netscape Navigator, and the integration of Internet Explorer into Windows in a way that made it difficult for users to remove or use alternative browsers.

In 2000, Judge Thomas Penfield Jackson issued his ruling, finding that Microsoft had indeed violated antitrust laws by engaging in anti-competitive practices. As a remedy, Judge Jackson ordered that Microsoft be broken up into two separate companies: one that would focus on the Windows operating system and another that would handle Microsoft's other software products, including Internet Explorer.

The Appeal and Settlement: Microsoft immediately appealed the ruling, and the case was eventually reviewed by the U.S. Court of Appeals for the D.C. Circuit. In 2001, the appeals court upheld the finding that Microsoft had engaged in anti-competitive practices, but it reversed the order to break up the company, arguing that the remedy was too extreme.

Instead of a breakup, the case was settled through a consent decree in 2001. Under the terms of the settlement, Microsoft agreed to several key concessions:

1. **Disclosure of APIs:** Microsoft was required to disclose technical information about its Application Programming Interfaces (APIs) to third-party developers, allowing them to create software that could interoperate with Windows in the same way as Microsoft's own products.

2. **Restrictions on Exclusive Deals:** Microsoft agreed to refrain from entering into exclusive agreements with PC manufacturers that would prevent them from installing competing software on their systems.

3. **Unbundling of Internet Explorer:** Microsoft was required to offer PC manufacturers the option to install Windows without bundling Internet Explorer, giving them more flexibility to include alternative browsers.

While the settlement fell short of the government's original goal of breaking up Microsoft, it imposed significant restrictions on the company's business practices and set a precedent for how antitrust law would be applied in the technology industry.

The Global Impact: The U.S. antitrust case against Microsoft was followed by similar actions in other countries. In 2004, the European Commission fined Microsoft for abusing its dominant market position and ordered the company to offer a version of Windows without Windows Media Player. The European Union also required Microsoft to provide users with a "browser ballot" in Windows, allowing them to choose from a range of web browsers instead of defaulting to Internet Explorer.

These legal challenges had a lasting impact on Microsoft and the broader technology industry. They underscored the importance of competition in fostering innovation and consumer choice, and they established important legal precedents that continue to influence antitrust enforcement in the tech sector.

The Lasting Impact of Windows 95 on Personal Computing and Internet Access

Revolutionizing the User Experience: Windows 95 is widely regarded as one of the most influential operating systems in the history of personal computing. Its introduction of the Start menu, taskbar, and desktop **interface** fundamentally changed how users interacted with their computers. Windows 95 made personal computing more accessible to the general public by offering a more intuitive and user-friendly interface compared to previous versions of Windows and other operating systems like MS-DOS.

The Start menu, in particular, became an iconic feature of Windows 95, allowing users to easily access programs, documents, and system settings from a single, centralized location. The taskbar provided a simple way to switch between open applications, making multitasking easier and more efficient. Together, these features helped to popularize the graphical user interface (GUI) as the standard for personal computing, moving away from the command-line interfaces that had dominated earlier systems.

Driving the Adoption of the Internet: Windows 95 played a critical role in driving the widespread adoption of the internet. The operating system's built-in support for the TCP/IP protocol made it easier for users to connect to the internet without needing to install additional software or configure complex settings. This seamless integration of internet connectivity was a significant factor in the rapid growth of internet usage during the mid-1990s.

The inclusion of Internet Explorer with Windows 95 further facilitated access to the World Wide Web. For many users, Internet Explorer was their first introduction to web browsing, and the convenience of having a pre-installed browser lowered the barrier to entry for exploring the internet. As a result, Windows 95 helped to democratize access to the internet, making it accessible to a broader audience and contributing to the explosive growth of online services and content.

Shaping the Future of Software Development: Windows 95 also had a profound impact on software development, both for Microsoft and the broader industry. The operating system introduced a more robust and flexible platform for developers, with improved support for 32-bit applications, better memory management, and a more stable architecture compared to earlier versions of Windows.

The success of Windows 95 encouraged developers to create software specifically for the Windows platform, leading to a vast ecosystem of applications that catered to a wide range of user needs. This ecosystem further solidified Windows' dominance in the personal computing market, as users were drawn to the platform's extensive library of software.

Moreover, Windows 95's widespread adoption helped to establish standards for software development that continue to influence the industry today. The operating system's use of the Windows API and the promotion of a consistent user interface across applications set expectations for how software should behave and interact with the operating system, laying the groundwork for future versions of Windows and other operating systems.

Legacy and Influence: The legacy of Windows 95 is evident in the continued dominance of the Windows operating system in the personal computing market. Many of the features and design principles introduced in Windows 95 have persisted through subsequent versions of Windows, including the Start menu, taskbar, and desktop interface. Even as technology has evolved and new platforms have emerged, the influence of Windows 95 on the way people interact with computers remains significant.

Windows 95 also played a key role in shaping the broader technology landscape. Its impact on the internet, software development, and user experience set the stage for the digital revolution that would follow in the late 1990s and early 2000s.

The operating system's success demonstrated the importance of making technology accessible and user-friendly, a principle that continues to drive innovation in the tech industry.

The Enduring Impact of the Browser Wars: The browser wars between Internet Explorer and Netscape had a lasting impact on the web and the software industry. The competition spurred rapid innovation in web technologies, leading to the development of more powerful and feature-rich browsers. However, the browser wars also highlighted the dangers of monopolistic practices and the importance of maintaining competition in the technology sector.

The antitrust cases against Microsoft served as a cautionary tale for other tech companies, reinforcing the need to balance innovation with fair competition. The legal precedents set by these cases continue to influence antitrust enforcement in the tech industry, particularly as new challenges arise in the era of big tech and digital monopolies.

The outcome of the browser wars also paved the way for the emergence of new browsers and platforms. The decline of Netscape led to the rise of the Mozilla project and the eventual creation of Firefox, which remains a popular alternative to mainstream browsers. Meanwhile, the lessons learned from the browser wars have informed the development of modern browsers like Google Chrome, which prioritize speed, security, and adherence to web standards.

Conclusion

Windows 95 and Internet Explorer had a profound and lasting impact on the personal computing and internet landscape. The bundling of Internet Explorer with Windows 95 was a strategic move that reshaped the browser market and sparked the intense competition of the browser wars. While Microsoft's aggressive tactics led to significant legal challenges and antitrust cases, the influence of Windows 95 on the accessibility and adoption of the internet cannot be overstated.

Windows 95 revolutionized personal computing by introducing a user-friendly interface that made technology more accessible to the general public. Its seamless integration of internet connectivity helped to democratize access to the World Wide Web, contributing to the rapid growth of online services and content. The operating system's success also set new standards for software development and established the foundations for the modern computing experience.

The legacy of Windows 95 and the browser wars continues to shape the technology industry today. The principles of user-centered design, open standards, and fair competition that emerged from this era remain central to the ongoing evolution of the internet and personal computing. As we look back on the history of technology, it is clear that Windows 95 and Internet Explorer were pivotal in driving the digital revolution that has transformed the world.

CHAPTER 13: THE DAWN OF HIGH-SPEED INTERNET

Overview

This chapter examines the pivotal transition from dial-up to broadband internet and its transformative impact on how people used the internet. We will explore the limitations of dial-up connections, the growing demand for faster speeds, the introduction of DSL (Digital Subscriber Line) and cable internet services, and how high-speed internet enabled new online experiences such as streaming and online gaming. Additionally, this chapter will feature interviews with early broadband users and service providers, offering personal insights into this technological revolution.

The Limitations of Dial-Up Connections and the Demand for Faster Speeds

The Era of Dial-Up Internet: In the early days of the internet, most users connected to the web through dial-up connections, which relied on standard telephone lines to transmit data. Dial-up modems converted digital data into analog signals that could be sent over the phone network. These connections typically offered speeds ranging from 28.8 kbps to 56 kbps, which were adequate for basic tasks like browsing text-based websites, sending emails, and downloading small files.

However, the limitations of dial-up quickly became apparent as the internet evolved and the demand for richer, more data-intensive content grew. Dial-up connections were notoriously slow, with long load times for websites, frequent disconnections, and the inability to use the phone line for voice calls while connected to the internet. As web pages began to include more images, audio, and video content, the need for faster internet speeds became increasingly urgent.

Growing Frustration and the Need for Speed: The frustrations associated with dial-up internet were a common experience for users in the 1990s. Waiting several minutes for a single webpage to load or enduring choppy, pixelated video streams was the norm. This slow, unreliable connectivity limited the scope of what users could do online and often discouraged them from engaging in more data-intensive activities.

The growing popularity of online gaming, multimedia websites, and early streaming services further highlighted the inadequacies of dial-up. Gamers found it challenging to play online multiplayer games due to high latency and frequent disconnections, while the emergence of platforms like Napster and RealPlayer demonstrated the need for faster download speeds and more stable connections.

As a result, there was a clear demand for faster, more reliable internet connections that could support the burgeoning digital content landscape. Users were eager for a solution that would enable them to fully experience the potential of the internet without the limitations imposed by dial-up technology.

The Introduction of DSL and Cable Internet Services

The Arrival of DSL: Digital Subscriber Line (DSL) technology emerged in the late 1990s as one of the first widely available broadband internet services. Unlike dial-up, which used the entire bandwidth of a telephone line, DSL utilized higher-frequency bands on the same line, allowing for data transmission without interfering with voice calls. This meant that users could be online and use the phone simultaneously—a significant improvement over dial-up.

DSL offered much higher speeds than dial-up, with early versions providing download speeds ranging from 256 kbps to 1.5 Mbps, depending on the quality of the phone line and the distance from the service provider's central office. These speeds were a substantial leap forward, enabling users to load web pages almost instantly, download files more quickly, and engage in more data-intensive activities.

The Rise of Cable Internet: Around the same time, cable internet services began to emerge as a competing broadband option. Cable internet leveraged the existing infrastructure of cable television networks to deliver high-speed internet access. By using the same coaxial cables that provided TV service, cable internet could offer even faster speeds than DSL, with early services delivering download speeds of up to 10 Mbps or more.

Cable internet quickly gained popularity in urban and suburban areas where cable TV networks were already well-established. The higher speeds and reliability of cable internet made it particularly attractive to users who were frustrated with the limitations of dial-up and eager for a faster, more seamless online experience.

Broadband Availability and Adoption: The rollout of DSL and cable internet services varied by region, with urban areas typically receiving access first due to the existing infrastructure. In rural areas, where telephone lines were often longer and of lower quality, DSL service was more limited, and the lack of cable TV networks meant that cable internet was often unavailable.

Despite these challenges, the availability of broadband internet expanded rapidly throughout the late 1990s and early 2000s. As service providers invested in infrastructure upgrades and new technologies, more households gained access to high-speed internet, leading to widespread adoption.

The transition from dial-up to broadband was a gradual process, with many users initially hesitant to switch due to the higher cost of broadband service. However, as prices dropped and the advantages of broadband became clear, the shift accelerated, and by the mid-2000s, broadband had largely supplanted dial-up as the standard for home internet access.

How High-Speed Internet Enabled New Online Experiences

The Rise of Streaming Media: One of the most significant impacts of high-speed internet was the emergence of streaming media. Streaming video and audio required a stable and fast connection, something that dial-up could not provide. With the advent of broadband, streaming became a viable option, allowing users to watch videos, listen to music, and even stream live events in real-time.

Services like YouTube, launched in 2005, and Netflix's streaming service, which debuted in 2007, revolutionized the way people consumed media. High-speed internet made it possible to stream content without lengthy buffering times, and users could watch videos in high quality, transforming their entertainment experiences. Music streaming services like Spotify, which launched in 2008, also benefited from broadband, enabling users to listen to entire libraries of music on demand.

The Evolution of Online Gaming: High-speed internet also had a profound impact on online gaming. Multiplayer games that were previously plagued by lag and disconnections on dial-up connections became much more enjoyable on broadband. Gamers could participate in fast-paced, real-time online games with players from around the world, fostering the growth of online gaming communities.

The increased bandwidth provided by broadband allowed for more complex and graphically rich games to be played online. This led to the rise of massively multiplayer online games (MMOs) like World of Warcraft, which launched in 2004 and became a cultural phenomenon. Broadband internet enabled these games to offer immersive experiences, with vast virtual worlds, real-time interactions, and a seamless connection to other players.

Expanding E-Commerce and Online Services: Broadband internet also contributed to the expansion of e-commerce and online services. Faster connections meant that websites could be more dynamic and feature-rich, with high-resolution images, interactive elements, and faster loading times. This made online shopping more appealing and convenient for consumers, leading to the growth of e-commerce giants like Amazon and eBay.

Online banking, video conferencing, and cloud-based services also benefited from broadband, as businesses and consumers could now access these services quickly and reliably. The increased bandwidth and reliability of broadband connections made it possible for companies to offer a wide range of online services, transforming industries and changing the way people worked, shopped, and communicated.

The Growth of Social Media: The rise of broadband internet coincided with the emergence of social media platforms. High-speed connections allowed users to easily share photos, videos, and other content on platforms like Facebook, which launched in 2004, and Twitter, which debuted in 2006. The ability to quickly upload and view multimedia content was a key factor in the rapid growth of social media, as users could now engage with richer and more diverse forms of communication.

Broadband also enabled the development of video-based social platforms, such as YouTube, where users could share and watch videos from around the world. The ease of access to high-quality video content helped to create a new generation of content creators and influencers, shaping the future of digital media and communication.

Interviews with Early Broadband Users and Service Providers

Voices from Early Broadband Adopters: To understand the impact of the transition from dial-up to broadband, we spoke with several early adopters who experienced the shift firsthand.

Karen Mitchell, a graphic designer from San Francisco, recalled the excitement of upgrading to broadband in the early 2000s. "Before broadband, I would spend hours waiting for files to download or webpages to load. It was frustrating, especially when I was working on projects that required a lot of online research. When I finally switched to DSL, it was like night and day. Suddenly, everything was faster, and I could get my work done so much more efficiently."

John Peterson, an avid gamer from Chicago, shared how broadband transformed his online gaming experience. "Playing games on dial-up was a nightmare—constant lag, disconnections, you name it. But when I got cable internet, it was a game-changer. I could finally play online without any issues, and I started connecting with gamers from all over the world. It really opened up a whole new world of gaming for me."

Insights from Service Providers: Service providers played a crucial role in the rollout of broadband internet, and we spoke with several industry veterans who were involved in the early days of broadband deployment.

Susan Harding, a former executive at a major DSL provider, discussed the challenges of bringing broadband to underserved areas. "In the beginning, our focus was on urban and suburban markets where the infrastructure was already in place. But as demand grew, we had to figure out how to deliver broadband to more rural areas, where the phone lines were older and longer. It was a challenge, but we knew that broadband was the future, and we were committed to making it available to as many people as possible."

Tom Blake, a network engineer at a cable company during the early 2000s, reflected on the technical innovations that enabled the growth of cable internet. "One of the biggest breakthroughs was DOCSIS (Data Over Cable Service Interface Specification), which allowed us to deliver high-speed internet over **existing cable television networks.** DOCSIS was a game-changer because it enabled us to offer broadband speeds that were significantly faster than what was possible with DSL at the time. It also allowed us to scale up our services quickly and reach more customers, especially in densely populated areas. The technology continued to evolve, and with each new version of DOCSIS, we were able to offer even higher speeds and better reliability."

Blake also highlighted the competitive environment that spurred innovation and improvement in broadband services. "There was a lot of competition between cable and DSL providers, which was great for consumers because it pushed us all to improve our services and lower prices. We were constantly looking for ways to enhance the customer experience, whether it was by increasing speeds, improving customer service, or offering new features like bundled TV and internet packages."

The Consumer Shift to Broadband: One of the most significant aspects of the broadband revolution was how it changed consumer expectations and behavior. As users experienced the benefits of high-speed internet, their usage patterns evolved dramatically.

Lisa Armstrong, a communications professor who conducted research on internet usage during the early 2000s, explained the psychological shift that occurred as people moved from dial-up to broadband. "Broadband fundamentally changed the way people interacted with the internet. With dial-up, users were often cautious about their online time because it was slow, and many had to share the phone line with other household members. But with broadband, the internet became something you could leave on all the time. This 'always-on' nature of broadband led to more frequent, casual, and integrated use of the internet in daily life. It changed the internet from a tool that you used occasionally to something that was part of your everyday routine."

Armstrong also noted how broadband influenced the development of internet-based businesses and services. "The availability of high-speed internet was a catalyst for the growth of online businesses. Companies that relied on heavy data transfer, like streaming services, cloud computing, and e-commerce platforms, were able to thrive because broadband made their services more accessible and user-friendly. This, in turn, led to the internet becoming an indispensable part of the global economy."

Conclusion

The transition from dial-up to broadband internet was a pivotal moment in the history of the internet, one that transformed how people used and experienced the online world. The limitations of dial-up connections created a demand for faster, more reliable internet services, which was met by the introduction of DSL and cable internet. These high-speed connections not only improved the user experience but also opened the door to new online activities and industries.

Broadband internet enabled the rise of streaming media, online gaming, and social media platforms, which have become central to modern life. It also facilitated the growth of e-commerce and online services, transforming how businesses operate and how people shop, communicate, and entertain themselves. The rapid adoption of broadband marked the beginning of an "always-on" internet culture, where the web became an integral part of daily life.

The interviews with early broadband users and service providers offer valuable insights into the challenges and triumphs of this technological shift. From overcoming technical obstacles to navigating competitive markets, the rollout of broadband internet was a complex and transformative process that has left a lasting legacy on the digital landscape.

As we look back on the dawn of high-speed internet, it is clear that this transition was more than just a technological upgrade—it was a fundamental change in the way we connect with the world, laying the foundation for the hyper-connected society we live in today.

CHAPTER 14: THE SOCIAL WEB EMERGES

Overview

This chapter explores the rise of social media and online communities in the early 2000s, marking a significant shift from traditional Bulletin Board Systems (BBSs) and forums to more dynamic social media platforms. We will examine the launch and growth of pioneering social networks like Friendster, MySpace, and Facebook, and discuss how these platforms fundamentally changed the way people interact online. Additionally, we will delve into the cultural and societal impacts of the social web, including its influence on communication, identity, and community building.

The Transition from BBSs and Forums to Social Media Platforms

The Legacy of BBSs and Forums: Before the advent of social media, online communities were primarily formed around Bulletin Board Systems (BBSs), forums, and newsgroups. These platforms provided spaces for users to engage in discussions, share information, and build communities around shared interests. While BBSs and forums were decentralized and often focused on specific topics or communities, they laid the groundwork for the development of more centralized and user-friendly social media platforms.

BBSs, such as FidoNet, were popular in the 1980s and early 1990s, allowing users to connect to local servers via dial-up connections. Forums and newsgroups, often hosted on early internet platforms like Usenet, allowed users to post messages and engage in threaded discussions. These early online communities were typically text-based, with limited graphical interfaces, and required a certain level of technical knowledge to navigate.

Despite their limitations, BBSs and forums were highly influential in shaping the early internet culture. They fostered a sense of community and belonging, allowing users to connect with others who shared their interests, regardless of geographic location. However, as internet access became more widespread and the web evolved, there was a growing demand for more sophisticated and accessible platforms that could connect people on a larger scale.

The Emergence of Social Media Platforms: The early 2000s saw the emergence of a new generation of online platforms designed to facilitate social interaction on a much larger scale than BBSs and forums. These platforms, known as social media, combined elements of online communities with user-friendly interfaces and rich multimedia features, making it easier for people to connect, share, and communicate.

One of the earliest social media platforms was Friendster, launched in 2002. Friendster was designed as a social networking service where users could create profiles, list their friends, and share content such as photos and status updates. Friendster introduced the concept of the "social graph," which mapped out the connections between users, allowing people to see how they were connected to others through mutual friends. This feature became a hallmark of social media, as it encouraged users to expand their networks and discover new connections.

Friendster's success demonstrated the potential of social media to attract a large and diverse user base. However, it was soon surpassed by MySpace, which launched in 2003 and quickly became the dominant social networking site of its time. MySpace offered a more customizable user experience, allowing users to personalize their profiles with music, videos, and custom HTML designs. This level of customization, combined with the platform's focus on music and pop culture, made MySpace particularly popular among younger users and aspiring musicians.

The rise of these early social media platforms marked a significant shift in the way people interacted online. Unlike the text-based and topic-specific communities of BBSs and forums, social media platforms were designed to facilitate personal connections and self-expression on a global scale. They provided users with the tools to create digital identities, share their lives with others, and build social networks that extended far beyond their immediate communities.

The Launch and Growth of Sites Like Friendster, MySpace, and Facebook

Friendster: The Pioneer of Social Networking: Friendster was one of the first social media platforms to gain widespread popularity, attracting millions of users within its first year. Founded by Jonathan Abrams, Friendster was designed to help people connect with friends and meet new people online. The platform's social graph feature allowed users to visualize their network of connections, making it easier to see how they were linked to others through mutual friends.

Despite its early success, Friendster faced significant challenges as it struggled to scale its technology infrastructure to accommodate its rapidly growing user base. Frequent technical issues, including slow load times and server crashes, led to frustration among users and ultimately contributed to the platform's decline. By the mid-2000s, many of Friendster's users had migrated to newer social media platforms that offered a more reliable and feature-rich experience.

MySpace: The Rise of a Cultural Phenomenon: MySpace,

launched in 2003 by Tom Anderson and Chris DeWolfe, quickly became a cultural phenomenon, particularly among teenagers and young adults. MySpace offered a level of customization that was unmatched by other social media platforms at the time, allowing users to personalize their profiles with custom backgrounds, music, and videos. This emphasis on self-expression and creativity resonated with users, making MySpace the go-to platform for social networking in the mid-2000s.

MySpace also played a significant role in the music industry, providing a platform for independent musicians to promote their work and connect with fans. Many artists, including global superstars like Arctic Monkeys and Lily Allen, got their start on MySpace, using the platform to build their fan bases and gain exposure. This integration of music and social networking helped to solidify MySpace's position as the leading social media site of its time.

At its peak, MySpace was the most visited website in the United States, with over 100 million active users. However, the platform's dominance was short-lived, as it faced increasing competition from a new social media giant: Facebook.

Facebook: Redefining Social Media: Facebook, founded in 2004 by Mark Zuckerberg along with his college roommates, started as a social networking site for Harvard University students. It quickly expanded to other Ivy League schools and then to universities across the United States, eventually opening up to the general public in 2006. Unlike MySpace, which emphasized customization and entertainment, Facebook focused on a clean, minimalist design and a more structured approach to social networking.

One of Facebook's key innovations was the introduction of the News Feed in 2006, which provided users with a real-time stream of updates from their friends. This feature fundamentally changed the way people interacted on social media, shifting the focus from individual profiles to a continuous flow of content and interactions. The News Feed encouraged users to engage with the platform more frequently, sharing status updates, photos, and links with their network of friends.

Facebook also introduced the concept of "likes," which allowed users to express approval for content shared by others. This seemingly simple feature had a profound impact on online behavior, as it incentivized users to share content that would generate positive feedback and engagement from their peers. The introduction of Facebook's "like" button in 2009 became a defining feature of social media, influencing the design and functionality of other platforms.

Facebook's emphasis on real-name identities and structured profiles made it particularly appealing to users who wanted a more authentic and professional online presence. As the platform grew, it expanded its features to include groups, events, and third-party apps, making it a versatile tool for social networking, business, and entertainment.

By the late 2000s, Facebook had overtaken MySpace as the most popular social networking site in the world. Its user base expanded rapidly, reaching over 1 billion users by 2012. Facebook's success reshaped the social media landscape, setting new standards for user experience, engagement, and connectivity.

How Social Media Changed the Way People Interact Online

The Shift from Anonymity to Identity: One of the most significant changes brought about by social media was the shift from anonymous interactions to identity-based connections. On early internet platforms like BBSs and forums, users often interacted under pseudonyms or usernames, which allowed for a degree of anonymity. Social media platforms like Facebook, however, encouraged users to create profiles with their real names and personal information, making online interactions more personal and transparent.

This emphasis on identity changed the nature of online interactions, as users were now more likely to connect with people they knew in real life, such as friends, family members, and colleagues. Social media became a platform for maintaining and strengthening existing relationships, as well as for discovering and connecting with new people who shared similar interests.

The shift to identity-based interactions also had implications for privacy and self-presentation. Users became more conscious of how they presented themselves online, curating their profiles and content to reflect their personal brand or desired image. This new dynamic introduced the concept of "social media personas," where users carefully managed their online identities to align with social norms and expectations.

The Rise of Viral Content and Online Trends: Social media platforms revolutionized the way content was shared and consumed online. The ability to easily share links, videos, and images with a large network of friends and followers led to the rise of viral content—media that spread rapidly across the internet, often reaching millions of people within a short period.

Platforms like Facebook and Twitter played a crucial role in amplifying viral content, as their algorithms prioritized popular and engaging posts in users' feeds. This created a feedback loop where highly shareable content was more likely to go viral, leading to the proliferation of memes, challenges, and other online trends that defined the cultural landscape of the 2000s and beyond.

Viral content also had a significant impact on the media industry, as news organizations and marketers recognized the power of social media to drive traffic and engagement. The desire to create shareable content led to the rise of "clickbait" headlines and sensationalist news, as publishers sought to capture the attention of social media users and capitalize on the viral potential of their stories.

The Evolution of Online Communication: Social media fundamentally changed the way people communicated online. Platforms like Facebook **and Twitter introduced new forms of communication that were more immediate, informal, and interactive compared to traditional methods like email or forums.** Status updates, tweets, and posts allowed users to share their thoughts, activities, and opinions in real-time, fostering a continuous stream of dialogue and interaction.

This shift to more frequent and brief communications encouraged a new style of online discourse, characterized by short, snappy updates and quick responses. The rise of "microblogging" platforms like Twitter, which limited posts to 140 characters (later expanded to 280), exemplified this trend. The concise nature of tweets forced users to be more direct and creative with their messaging, leading to the development of new forms of expression, such as hashtags and emojis, which have since become integral parts of digital communication.

Social media also introduced new ways for people to engage with content and each other through features like comments, likes, shares, and reactions. These interactive elements made online communication more dynamic and participatory, as users could easily respond to and amplify the content shared by others. The public nature of these interactions also created a sense of community and collective engagement, as users could see and participate in conversations happening across their social networks.

The Impact on Relationships and Social Dynamics: The rise of social media had profound effects on relationships and social dynamics, both online and offline. By making it easier to stay in touch with friends, family, and acquaintances, social media strengthened existing relationships and created new opportunities for social connection. Users could share life updates, celebrate milestones, and offer support to one another, all within the digital space of their social networks.

However, the pervasive nature of social media also introduced new challenges and complexities to social interactions. The constant visibility of other people's lives through status updates and photos led to phenomena like "social comparison," where users compared their own lives to the often idealized portrayals of others. This could lead to feelings of inadequacy or envy, as people measured their success and happiness against the curated images and stories presented by their peers.

Social media also blurred the boundaries between different social circles, as users could connect with friends, family, colleagues, and even strangers on the same platform. This convergence of social spheres sometimes led to awkward or uncomfortable situations, as content intended for one group of people could be seen by others who might interpret it differently. The need to navigate these complex social dynamics prompted users to become more mindful of their online behavior and the way they presented themselves to different audiences.

The Role of Social Media in Shaping Public Discourse: As social media became a central part of daily life, it also emerged as a powerful platform for shaping public discourse. The ability to share news, opinions, and information with a broad audience gave social media users a voice in important social, political, and cultural conversations. Platforms like Facebook, Twitter, and YouTube became key arenas for public debate, activism, and the dissemination of ideas.

The rise of social media activism, sometimes referred to as "hashtag activism," demonstrated the potential of these platforms to mobilize large numbers of people around social and political causes. Campaigns like #BlackLivesMatter, #MeToo, and #ClimateStrike gained global attention through social media, highlighting issues of racial injustice, gender inequality, and environmental protection. These movements showed how social media could amplify marginalized voices, raise awareness of important issues, and drive social change.

However, the role of social media in public discourse also raised concerns about the spread of misinformation, echo chambers, and polarization. The algorithms that powered social media platforms often prioritized content that was sensational, controversial, or emotionally charged, which could contribute to the spread of false information and the entrenchment of divisive opinions. The public nature of social media also made it a fertile ground for online harassment, trolling, and the spread of extremist views, posing significant challenges to the health and integrity of public discourse.

The Cultural and Societal Impacts of the Social Web

The Transformation of Identity and Self-Expression: Social media has had a profound impact on how people perceive and express their identities. The ability to curate a digital persona allowed users to explore different aspects of themselves, experiment with self-presentation, and connect with others who shared similar interests or experiences. Platforms like Facebook, Instagram, and TikTok became spaces for creative self-expression, where users could share their thoughts, talents, and passions with a global audience.

The social web also played a key role in shaping the identities of younger generations, who grew up with social media as a central part of their lives. For many young people, social media became a primary means of communication and socialization, influencing their sense of self, relationships, and worldview. The pressure to maintain an attractive and engaging online presence sometimes led to challenges related to self-esteem, mental health, and the authenticity of online interactions.

At the same time, social media provided a platform for marginalized communities to find representation and support. LGBTQ+ individuals, people of color, and other underrepresented groups used social media to build communities, share their stories, and advocate for their rights. The visibility and connectivity offered by social media helped to foster greater acceptance and understanding of diverse identities and experiences, contributing to broader social and cultural change.

The Evolution of Consumer Culture: The rise of social media significantly influenced consumer culture, as platforms became key channels for marketing, advertising, and brand engagement. Social media enabled companies to connect directly with consumers, build brand communities, and leverage user-generated content to enhance their marketing efforts. The use of influencers—social media personalities with large followings—became a powerful tool for brands to reach target audiences and promote products in a more authentic and relatable way.

Social media also transformed the way consumers made purchasing decisions. Platforms like Instagram and Pinterest became popular sources of inspiration for fashion, home decor, travel, and other lifestyle choices. The integration of shopping features into social media apps allowed users to discover and purchase products directly within the platform, blurring the lines between content consumption and commerce.

The influence of social media on consumer behavior extended beyond individual purchases to broader trends and movements. Viral challenges, hashtag campaigns, and social media-driven trends shaped popular culture and influenced everything from fashion to food to social norms. The ability of social media to create and spread trends at lightning speed highlighted its role as a key driver of cultural change in the digital age.

The Impact on Privacy and Data Security: The widespread adoption of social media also raised significant concerns about privacy and data security. Social media platforms collected vast amounts of personal data from users, including their preferences, behaviors, and social connections. This data was often used for targeted advertising, algorithmic recommendations, and other purposes that benefited the platform and its advertisers.

The collection and use of personal data by social media companies led to growing awareness and concern about privacy rights and data protection. High-profile incidents, such as the Cambridge Analytica scandal, exposed how personal data could be misused for political manipulation and other unethical purposes. These revelations prompted calls for greater transparency, regulation, and accountability in how social media companies handle user data.

The tension between the benefits of social media and the risks to privacy and security remains a central issue in the digital age. Users continue to grapple with the trade-offs between the convenience and connectivity offered by social media and the potential loss of control over their personal information.

The Role of Social Media in Globalization: Social media played a significant role in accelerating the process of globalization by connecting people across borders and fostering cross-cultural exchange. Platforms like Facebook, Twitter, and YouTube enabled users to engage with content and individuals from around the world, facilitating the spread of ideas, trends, and movements on a global scale.

This global connectivity contributed to the emergence of a more interconnected and interdependent world, where information, culture, and commerce flowed freely across national boundaries. Social media became a key tool for global activism, as movements like the Arab Spring used platforms to organize protests, share information, and draw international attention to their causes.

However, the global reach of social media also highlighted disparities in access to technology and the internet. While social media connected people in urban and developed regions, many communities in rural and underdeveloped areas remained disconnected from the digital world. The digital divide raised questions about the inclusivity and equity of the social web, and efforts to bridge this gap became an important focus for governments, NGOs, and tech companies.

Conclusion

The emergence of the social web in the early 2000s marked a profound transformation in the way people interact, communicate, and engage with the world online. The transition from BBSs and forums to social media platforms like Friendster, MySpace, and Facebook introduced new forms of social connection and self-expression, reshaping personal relationships, identity, and public discourse.

Social media revolutionized online communication by introducing real-time, interactive, and identity-based interactions. It enabled the rise of viral content, social trends, and global movements, while also influencing consumer culture, privacy norms, and the dynamics of globalization. The cultural and societal impacts of the social web continue to unfold, as social media remains a powerful and evolving force in the digital age.

As we reflect on the rise of social media, it is clear that these platforms have fundamentally changed the way we connect with others, share information, and shape our identities. The social web has brought both opportunities and challenges, and its influence will continue to be felt for generations to come.

CHAPTER 15: THE INTERNET'S ROLE IN GLOBALIZATION

Overview

This chapter analyzes the profound role the internet has played in connecting the world and facilitating globalization. We will explore how the internet has transformed global communication and trade, contributed to the rise of e-commerce and its effects on traditional retail, influenced global culture and politics, and examine the challenges posed by the digital divide, as well as the efforts to provide global internet access.

The Internet's Impact on Global Communication and Trade

Revolutionizing Global Communication: The internet has fundamentally transformed global communication, breaking down barriers of distance and time. Before the advent of the internet, international communication was limited to slower, less reliable methods such as postal mail, expensive long-distance phone calls, and fax machines. The internet introduced a new era of instant communication, enabling people around the world to connect and interact in real-time through email, instant messaging, video conferencing, and social media.

This shift has had profound implications for both personal and professional communication. Families separated by geography can now stay in close contact through video calls and social media platforms, while businesses can collaborate with partners and clients across different continents with unprecedented ease. The internet has made the world feel smaller and more interconnected, fostering a global community where ideas, knowledge, and culture can be shared across borders almost instantaneously.

Facilitating Global Trade and Commerce: The internet has also revolutionized global trade, creating a more interconnected and efficient global economy. E-commerce platforms and online marketplaces have made it possible for businesses of all sizes to reach a global customer base, regardless of their physical location. Companies can now sell products and services to consumers in distant markets with just a few clicks, bypassing the traditional barriers of geography and time zones.

The rise of online payment systems, such as PayPal, Stripe, and various digital wallets, has facilitated cross-border transactions, making it easier for consumers to purchase goods and services from international sellers. Additionally, the internet has enabled the growth of global supply chains, allowing companies to source materials and manufacture products in different countries, optimizing for cost, quality, and speed.

One of the most significant impacts of the internet on global trade has been the emergence of a new class of "micro-multinationals"—small and medium-sized enterprises (SMEs) that leverage the internet to compete in global markets. These businesses can operate with minimal overhead costs, using e-commerce platforms, cloud-based services, and digital marketing to reach customers worldwide. This democratization of global trade has opened up new opportunities for entrepreneurs and has contributed to the growth of the global economy.

The Growth of Remote Work and Outsourcing: The internet has also enabled the rise of remote work and outsourcing, transforming the way businesses operate and manage their workforce. High-speed internet connections, video conferencing tools, and cloud-based collaboration platforms have made it possible for employees to work from anywhere, leading to the growth of remote work as a viable option for many professionals.

Outsourcing, particularly in industries like software development, customer service, and data entry, has become a common practice for businesses looking to reduce costs and access a global talent pool. The internet has made it easier for companies to outsource tasks to workers in other countries, often in regions with lower labor costs. This has led to the creation of new economic opportunities in developing countries, while also raising questions about job displacement and the impact on local labor markets in developed nations.

The Rise of E-Commerce and Its Effects on Traditional Retail

The Emergence of E-Commerce: E-commerce, or electronic commerce, refers to the buying and selling of goods and services over the internet. The rise of e-commerce has been one of the most transformative developments of the digital age, reshaping the retail landscape and changing the way consumers shop. The growth of e-commerce has been driven by several factors, including the increasing availability of high-speed internet, the proliferation of smartphones and other mobile devices, and the development of secure online payment systems.

Amazon, founded by Jeff Bezos in 1994 as an online bookstore, quickly expanded into other product categories and became the largest e-commerce platform in the world. Amazon's success demonstrated the potential of e-commerce to disrupt traditional retail, offering consumers a convenient, efficient, and often cheaper way to shop for a wide range of products. Other e-commerce giants, such as eBay, Alibaba, and Shopify, have also played significant roles in the growth of online retail, each offering unique platforms and services that cater to different markets and consumer needs.

The Impact on Traditional Retail: The rise of e-commerce has had profound effects on traditional brick-and-mortar retail. As more consumers turn to online shopping for its convenience and competitive pricing, traditional retailers have faced significant challenges in maintaining foot traffic and sales. Many brick-and-mortar stores have struggled to compete with the wide selection, ease of comparison, and personalized shopping experiences offered by e-commerce platforms.

The impact of e-commerce on traditional retail has been particularly pronounced in certain sectors, such as electronics, books, and apparel, where online shopping offers clear advantages in terms of price, selection, and convenience. In response, many traditional retailers have had to adapt by developing their own online sales channels, embracing omnichannel strategies that integrate physical stores with e-commerce, and enhancing their in-store experiences to attract customers.

The "retail apocalypse," a term used to describe the wave of store closures and bankruptcies among traditional retailers, has been partly attributed to the rise of e-commerce. While e-commerce has certainly disrupted the retail industry, it has also created new opportunities for businesses to innovate and reach customers in new ways. Many retailers have successfully navigated this shift by leveraging digital technologies, data analytics, and personalized marketing to stay competitive in the changing landscape.

The Future of Retail: The future of retail is likely to be shaped by a continued blending of online and offline experiences. Innovations such as augmented reality (AR), virtual reality (VR), and artificial intelligence (AI) are expected to further transform the shopping experience, offering consumers more immersive and personalized interactions with brands and products. Additionally, the rise of social commerce, where shopping is integrated into social media platforms, is creating new ways for consumers to discover and purchase products.

The COVID-19 pandemic accelerated the shift to e-commerce, as lockdowns and social distancing measures forced many consumers to shop online for the first time. This shift is expected to have lasting effects on consumer behavior, with e-commerce continuing to grow as a dominant force in the retail industry. However, the physical store is not expected to disappear entirely; instead, it will likely evolve to serve new functions, such as providing experiential shopping experiences, facilitating product returns, and acting as fulfillment centers for online orders.

How the Internet Has Influenced Global Culture and Politics

Cultural Globalization and the Spread of Ideas: The internet has played a central role in the process of cultural globalization, facilitating the rapid spread of ideas, values, and cultural practices across the world. Social media platforms, streaming services, and content-sharing sites have made it easier for people to access and share cultural content from different regions, leading to a greater exchange of ideas and the blending of cultural influences.

The rise of global platforms like YouTube, Netflix, and Spotify has allowed cultural products such as music, movies, TV shows, and viral videos to reach audiences far beyond their countries of origin. For example, the global popularity of K-pop, a genre of music originating from South Korea, can be attributed in large part to the internet's ability to connect fans and share content across borders. Similarly, the internet has helped to popularize international cuisines, fashion trends, and lifestyle practices, contributing to a more interconnected global culture.

However, the globalization of culture through the internet has also raised concerns about cultural homogenization and the potential loss of local traditions and identities. While the internet has enabled the spread of diverse cultural content, it has also facilitated the dominance of certain cultural products, particularly those from Western countries, leading to fears of a "cultural imperialism" that could erode local cultures.

The Internet as a Platform for Political Activism: The internet has also become a powerful tool for political activism, providing a platform for individuals and groups to organize, mobilize, and advocate for social and political change. Social media platforms, in particular, have played a critical role in amplifying the voices of activists, raising awareness of important issues, and facilitating grassroots movements.

The Arab Spring, a series of pro-democracy uprisings that took place across the Middle East and North Africa in the early 2010s, is often cited as a key example of the internet's influence on global politics. Activists used social media platforms like Facebook and Twitter to organize protests, share information, and document human rights abuses, helping to galvanize support for the movements and draw international attention to their causes.

The internet has also played a role in shaping public opinion and influencing elections, as seen in the spread of misinformation and propaganda during the 2016 U.S. presidential election and the Brexit referendum in the United Kingdom. The ability of social media platforms to amplify certain narratives, combined with the use of targeted advertising and data analytics, has raised concerns about the potential manipulation of public discourse and the impact on democratic processes.

The Challenge of Misinformation and Censorship: While the internet has facilitated the free flow of information and ideas, it has also created challenges related to misinformation, disinformation, and censorship. The rapid spread of false or misleading information online can have serious consequences, from undermining public trust in institutions to inciting violence and spreading harmful conspiracy theories.

Governments, tech companies, and civil society organizations have struggled to find effective ways to combat misinformation without infringing on freedom of speech. The challenge is particularly acute in countries with authoritarian regimes, where governments may use internet censorship and surveillance to suppress dissent and control the flow of information.

The global nature of the internet also complicates efforts to regulate content and protect users from harm. Different countries have different laws and norms related to free speech, privacy, and data protection , **making it difficult to implement consistent global standards for online content.** This lack of uniformity has led to conflicts between governments, tech companies, and international organizations as they navigate the complex landscape of internet governance.

In some regions, authoritarian governments have implemented extensive internet censorship regimes, using sophisticated tools to block access to certain websites, monitor online activities, and control the dissemination of information. Countries like China, Russia, and Iran have developed systems of online censorship that restrict access to global platforms and promote state-approved narratives. The Great Firewall of China, for example, is a comprehensive system of internet controls that blocks access to foreign websites and censors politically sensitive content.

At the same time, efforts to combat misinformation in democratic societies have raised concerns about the balance between security and civil liberties. Social media companies have faced criticism for both their failure to prevent the spread of harmful content and their perceived overreach in moderating speech. The debate over how to regulate online content while preserving freedom of expression remains one of the most pressing issues in the digital age.

The Digital Divide and Efforts to Provide Global Internet Access

Understanding the Digital Divide: Despite the transformative impact of the internet on global communication, trade, culture, and politics, not everyone has benefited equally from this technology. The "digital divide" refers to the gap between those who have access to the internet and digital technologies and those who do not. This divide can be observed both between countries (the global digital divide) and within countries (the domestic digital divide).

The global digital divide is particularly pronounced between developed and developing countries. In many parts of Africa, Asia, and Latin America, internet access is limited by factors such as inadequate infrastructure, high costs, and lack of digital literacy. Rural and remote areas are often the most affected, with populations that have limited or no access to high-speed internet. This lack of connectivity exacerbates existing inequalities, limiting access to information, education, healthcare, and economic opportunities.

The domestic digital divide, on the other hand, can be seen within countries, where certain populations—such as low-income households, older adults, and minority communities—are less likely to have access to the internet or the skills needed to use it effectively. This divide has significant implications for social and economic inclusion, as those without internet access are often left behind in the digital economy.

Efforts to Bridge the Digital Divide: Addressing the digital divide has become a priority for governments, international organizations, and private sector companies. Efforts to bridge the divide focus on expanding infrastructure, reducing costs, and increasing digital literacy.

1. **Infrastructure Development:** Expanding internet infrastructure in underserved areas is critical to closing the digital divide. Governments and telecommunications companies have invested in building broadband networks, laying undersea cables, and deploying satellite internet services to reach remote and rural communities. Initiatives like the "Digital India" campaign and the "AfricaConnect" project aim to bring high-speed internet to millions of people who currently lack access.

2. **Reducing Costs:** The cost of internet access remains a significant barrier for many people, particularly in developing countries. To address this, some governments have implemented policies to reduce the cost of internet services, such as subsidizing broadband deployment, regulating prices, and promoting competition among service providers. Additionally, initiatives like the "Free Basics" program by Facebook have sought to provide free access to a limited set of internet services, though these efforts have also sparked debates about net neutrality and digital rights.

3. **Increasing Digital Literacy:** Digital literacy—defined as the ability to use digital technologies effectively and safely—is essential for ensuring that people can fully participate in the digital world. Governments, non-profits, and educational institutions have launched programs to teach digital skills, from basic computer usage to more advanced topics like coding and cybersecurity. These programs are particularly important for reaching marginalized groups, such as older adults and low-income communities, who may be less familiar with digital technologies.

4. **Public-Private Partnerships:** Public-private partnerships have played a crucial role in efforts to expand internet access and bridge the digital divide. Companies like Google, Microsoft, and SpaceX have launched ambitious projects to provide global internet coverage through technologies like balloons, drones, and low-earth orbit satellites. These initiatives, such as Google's Project Loon and SpaceX's Starlink, aim to connect the most remote parts of the world to the internet.

The Role of International Organizations: International organizations such as the United Nations, the World Bank, and the International Telecommunication Union (ITU) have also been instrumental in efforts to bridge the digital divide. The UN's Sustainable Development Goals (SDGs), for example, include targets related to ensuring universal and affordable access to the internet by 2030. These organizations work with governments and the private sector to promote policies and investments that support digital inclusion and address the barriers to internet access.

Challenges and Future Outlook: While significant progress has been made in expanding internet access globally, challenges remain. The cost of deploying infrastructure in remote areas, regulatory hurdles, and geopolitical tensions can hinder efforts to close the digital divide. Additionally, as new technologies like 5G and AI become more prevalent, there is a risk that the digital divide could widen further, as those without access to these technologies are left behind.

Looking ahead, it is clear that addressing the digital divide will require continued collaboration between governments, the private sector, and civil society. Efforts to expand infrastructure, lower costs, and promote digital literacy must be sustained and scaled to ensure that everyone, regardless of location or socioeconomic status, can benefit from the opportunities provided by the internet.

Conclusion

The internet has been a driving force in the process of globalization, revolutionizing communication, trade, culture, and politics. It has connected people across the world in ways that were previously unimaginable, facilitating the exchange of ideas, goods, and services on a global scale. The rise of e-commerce, the spread of global culture, and the empowerment of political movements are just a few of the ways in which the internet has transformed our world.

However, the benefits of the internet have not been evenly distributed, and the digital divide remains a significant challenge. Bridging this divide is essential for ensuring that all people can participate in and benefit from the digital age. As we continue to navigate the complexities of internet governance, misinformation, and the challenges of global connectivity, it is clear that the internet's role in globalization will remain a central issue in the years to come.

The internet has the potential to bring us closer together, foster innovation, and create new opportunities for millions of people around the world. But realizing this potential will require a concerted effort to address the challenges and inequalities that persist in the digital landscape. As we move forward, the goal must be to create a more inclusive, equitable, and connected world where the benefits of the internet are accessible to all.

CHAPTER 16: THE DARK SIDE OF THE INTERNET

Overview

This chapter explores the darker aspects of the internet, focusing on the rise of cybercrime, privacy concerns, and the emergence of the dark web. We will examine the evolution of hacking and cyber warfare, the challenges of maintaining privacy and security online, the development and impact of the dark web, and the legal and ethical considerations that arise in the digital age.

The Emergence of Hacking and Cyber Warfare

The Evolution of Hacking: Hacking, in its earliest form, was often associated with curiosity and experimentation. In the 1960s and 1970s, the term "hacker" referred to skilled programmers and computer enthusiasts who sought to push the boundaries of technology. Early hacking was largely benign, focusing on exploring computer systems and networks without malicious intent. However, as computers and the internet became more integral to society, hacking evolved into a more dangerous activity, often associated with criminal behavior and malicious intent.

By the 1980s and 1990s, hacking had become more widespread and increasingly sophisticated. The advent of the internet provided new opportunities for hackers to exploit vulnerabilities in computer systems, leading to the rise of cybercrime. Notable incidents during this period include the creation of the Morris Worm in 1988, one of the first internet-based worms, and the rise of hacker groups like the Chaos Computer Club and the Legion of Doom, who gained notoriety for their exploits.

As the internet grew, so did the scale and impact of hacking. Cybercriminals began to target financial institutions, government agencies, and large corporations, stealing sensitive data, disrupting services, and causing significant financial and reputational damage. The motivations for hacking became more diverse, ranging from financial gain and political activism to espionage and cyberterrorism.

The Rise of Cyber Warfare: Cyber warfare refers to the use of digital attacks by nation-states or non-state actors to disrupt, damage, or gain control of information systems, critical infrastructure, or other assets of strategic importance. As governments and militaries around the world have become increasingly reliant on digital technology, the threat of cyber warfare has emerged as a significant concern in national and international security.

One of the earliest examples of cyber warfare was the 2007 cyberattacks on Estonia, a NATO member state. The attacks, which targeted government, financial, and media websites, were widely attributed to Russian hackers, although no direct link to the Russian government was officially established. The incident highlighted the vulnerability of modern societies to cyberattacks and marked the beginning of a new era of digital conflict.

The Stuxnet worm, discovered in 2010, is another notable example of cyber warfare. Stuxnet was a highly sophisticated piece of malware designed to target and sabotage Iran's nuclear enrichment facilities. The worm, which is believed to have been developed by the United States and Israel, demonstrated the potential for cyber weapons to cause physical damage to critical infrastructure.

In recent years, cyber warfare has become a key component of geopolitical conflict, with nation-states increasingly using cyberattacks to achieve strategic objectives. This includes attempts to disrupt elections, conduct espionage, and disable critical infrastructure. The rise of cyber warfare has prompted governments to develop new strategies and capabilities to defend against digital threats, leading to the establishment of cyber defense units and the integration of cyber operations into military planning.

Hacktivism and Cyber Terrorism: Hacktivism, a blend of hacking and activism, involves the use of hacking techniques to promote political or social causes. Hacktivist groups, such as Anonymous and LulzSec, have gained attention for their high-profile attacks on government agencies, corporations, and other organizations they deem to be acting unethically. These attacks often involve website defacements, data breaches, and distributed denial-of-service (DDoS) attacks designed to disrupt operations and draw attention to their cause.

Cyber terrorism, on the other hand, involves the use of digital attacks to instill fear, cause disruption, or achieve political or ideological goals. Unlike hacktivists, who may seek to raise awareness or protest specific issues, cyber terrorists aim to cause widespread harm and panic. The potential for cyber terrorism has raised concerns about the security of critical infrastructure, such as power grids, transportation systems, and financial networks, which could be targeted by terrorists seeking to inflict maximum damage.

The Challenges of Maintaining Privacy and Security Online

The Growing Threat of Data Breaches: As the internet has become an integral part of daily life, the amount of personal and sensitive information stored online has increased exponentially. This has made data breaches a significant threat to individuals, businesses, and governments. Data breaches occur when unauthorized individuals gain access to sensitive data, such as personal information, financial records, or intellectual property.

Major data breaches have affected some of the world's largest companies and institutions, exposing the personal information of millions of users. Notable examples include the 2013 Target breach, in which the credit and debit card information of over 40 million customers was compromised, and the 2017 Equifax breach, which exposed the personal data of 147 million people.

Data breaches can have severe consequences, including financial loss, identity theft, and damage to reputation. For businesses, the cost of a data breach can be substantial, both in terms of direct financial losses and the long-term impact on customer trust and loyalty. For individuals, the loss of personal information can lead to identity theft, fraud, and other forms of cybercrime.

Surveillance and the Erosion of Privacy: The rise of the internet has also brought about new challenges related to surveillance and the erosion of privacy. Governments, corporations, and other entities now have unprecedented access to individuals' personal data, often without their knowledge or consent. This has led to widespread concerns about the extent to which privacy is being compromised in the digital age.

Government surveillance programs, such as those revealed by former NSA contractor Edward Snowden in 2013, have sparked significant debate about the balance between national security and individual privacy. The Snowden leaks exposed the extent to which governments were collecting and analyzing data on their own citizens and foreign nationals, often with little oversight or transparency. The revelations led to global discussions about the need for stronger privacy protections and the potential abuse of surveillance powers.

In addition to government surveillance, the rise of data-driven business models has led to the widespread collection and monetization of personal information by corporations.

Companies like Google, Facebook, and Amazon collect vast amounts of data on their users' behavior, preferences, and interactions, which they use to target advertising and optimize their services. While these practices have driven significant innovation and economic growth, they have also raised concerns about the loss of privacy and the potential for misuse of personal data.

The Challenge of Securing Online Identities: As more aspects of life move online, securing digital identities has become increasingly important. Passwords, once the primary means of securing online accounts, are now widely recognized as insufficient to protect against modern threats. Weak passwords, password reuse, and phishing attacks have made it easier for cybercriminals to gain access to user accounts and personal information.

To address these challenges, many organizations have implemented multi-factor authentication (MFA), which requires users to provide additional verification, such as a code sent to their mobile device, in addition to their password. Biometric authentication methods, such as fingerprint and facial recognition, have also become more common as a means of securing online identities.

However, securing online identities is an ongoing challenge, as cybercriminals continue to develop new techniques to bypass security measures. Social engineering attacks, such as phishing and spear-phishing, remain a significant threat, as they exploit human vulnerabilities rather than technical flaws. As the internet continues to evolve, the need for robust security measures to protect online identities will remain a critical concern.

The Development and Impact of the Dark Web

What Is the Dark Web? The dark web is a part of the internet that is not indexed by traditional search engines and can only be accessed using specialized software, such as the Tor browser. Unlike the surface web, which is publicly accessible and searchable, the dark web is intentionally hidden, providing a high degree of anonymity for its users. While the dark web is often associated with illegal activities, it also serves as a platform for privacy-focused communications and the exchange of information in regions with heavy censorship.

The dark web is a subset of the deep web, which refers to all parts of the internet that are not indexed by search engines. The deep web includes a wide range of legitimate content, such as private databases, academic journals, and subscription-based services. The dark web, however, is specifically designed to be hidden and anonymous, making it a haven for illegal activities.

The Rise of Dark Web Marketplaces: One of the most notorious aspects of the dark web is the presence of online marketplaces that facilitate the trade of illegal goods and services. These marketplaces operate similarly to e-commerce sites on the surface web, but they allow users to buy and sell items such as drugs, weapons, counterfeit documents, and stolen data with a high degree of anonymity.

Silk Road, launched in 2011, was one of the first and most well-known dark web marketplaces. It operated as a black market for drugs and other illegal goods, using Bitcoin to facilitate anonymous transactions. The site was eventually shut down by the FBI in 2013, and its founder, Ross Ulbricht, was arrested and sentenced to life in prison. Despite its closure, Silk Road set a precedent for other dark web marketplaces, which have since proliferated.

These marketplaces pose significant challenges for law enforcement, as the anonymity provided by the dark web makes it difficult to trace transactions and identify the individuals involved. While some marketplaces have been shut down by authorities, others continue to emerge, adapting to new security measures and law enforcement tactics.

The Dark Web's Role in Cybercrime: The dark web is also a hub for various forms of cybercrime, including the sale of hacking tools, malware, and stolen data.

Cybercriminals use the dark web to buy and sell tools and services that can be used to carry out attacks on individuals, businesses, and governments. These include everything from ransomware and phishing kits to zero-day exploits and botnet rentals. The dark web also provides a marketplace for stolen personal information, such as credit card numbers, Social Security numbers, and login credentials, which can be used for identity theft and financial fraud.

The anonymity of the dark web makes it a preferred platform for cybercriminals to exchange information, plan attacks, and collaborate on illegal activities. Forums and chat rooms on the dark web serve as meeting places where hackers can share knowledge, recruit members, and discuss strategies. This has contributed to the rise of organized cybercrime, with criminal groups operating across borders and conducting large-scale, coordinated attacks.

One of the most significant threats emerging from the dark web is ransomware-as-a-service (RaaS). This model allows less technically skilled criminals to launch ransomware attacks by purchasing or renting the necessary tools from more experienced hackers. The rise of RaaS has led to an increase in the frequency and sophistication of ransomware attacks, which have targeted everything from small businesses to critical infrastructure.

The Impact on Society and Law Enforcement: The activities on the dark web have had a profound impact on society, particularly in terms of the challenges they pose to law enforcement. The anonymous nature of the dark web makes it difficult for authorities to identify and apprehend criminals, leading to a cat-and-mouse game between law enforcement agencies and cybercriminals.

Despite these challenges, law enforcement agencies have had some success in infiltrating and dismantling dark web marketplaces and forums. Operations like the takedown of

Silk Road, AlphaBay, and Hansa Market have shown that it is possible to disrupt illegal activities on the dark web, though new marketplaces often emerge to take their place.

In addition to law enforcement efforts, there have been calls for greater regulation of cryptocurrencies, which are often used to facilitate transactions on the dark web. The anonymous nature of cryptocurrencies like Bitcoin makes them attractive to criminals, but it also complicates efforts to track and prevent illegal transactions. Some governments have introduced regulations requiring cryptocurrency exchanges to implement Know Your Customer (KYC) protocols and report suspicious activities, though the effectiveness of these measures is still being debated.

The dark web also raises ethical and legal questions about privacy, surveillance, and the balance between security and civil liberties. While the dark web is often associated with illegal activities, it is also used by journalists, activists, and whistleblowers in repressive regimes to communicate and share information anonymously. This has led to debates about the extent to which law enforcement should be allowed to monitor and intervene in the dark web, and how to protect legitimate users while combating criminal activity.

Legal and Ethical Considerations in the Digital Age

Balancing Security and Privacy: One of the central challenges in the digital age is balancing the need for security with the protection of individual privacy. Governments and law enforcement agencies argue that surveillance and data collection are necessary to prevent cybercrime, terrorism, and other threats. However, these measures often come at the cost of personal privacy and civil liberties, raising concerns about government overreach and the potential for abuse.

The debate over encryption is a key example of this tension. Encryption is a fundamental tool for protecting data and communications from unauthorized access, but it also makes it more difficult for law enforcement to investigate criminal activity. Governments in several countries have pushed for backdoors in encryption systems, which would allow them to access encrypted data with a warrant. However, privacy advocates and technology companies argue that such backdoors would weaken security for everyone and could be exploited by malicious actors.

The legal landscape surrounding digital privacy is constantly evolving, with new laws and regulations being introduced to address the challenges of the digital age. The European Union's General Data Protection Regulation (GDPR), which came into effect in 2018, is one of the most comprehensive data protection laws in the world, setting strict guidelines for how companies collect, store, and use personal data. Other countries have introduced similar regulations, though the level of protection varies widely.

The Ethics of Data Collection and Usage: The widespread collection and use of personal data by corporations raise significant ethical questions. While data-driven business models have enabled the growth of personalized services, targeted advertising, and improved user experiences, they have also led to concerns about the erosion of privacy and the potential for data misuse.

One of the major ethical dilemmas is the concept of informed consent. Many users are unaware of the extent to which their data is being collected, how it is being used, and who it is being shared with. Privacy policies are often lengthy, complex, and difficult to understand, leading to a situation where users may unknowingly consent to practices that they might find unacceptable if they were fully informed.

The issue of data ownership is another ethical concern. As companies collect and monetize user data, questions arise about who truly owns that data and how much control individuals should have over their personal information. The concept of "data sovereignty" has gained traction, with advocates calling for greater rights and protections for individuals in how their data is used.

The rise of big data and AI has also raised concerns about bias and discrimination. Algorithms that process vast amounts of data can inadvertently reinforce existing biases, leading to unfair outcomes in areas such as hiring, lending, and law enforcement. The lack of transparency in how these algorithms work further complicates efforts to address these issues.

Legal Responses to Cybercrime and Cyber Warfare: The rise of cybercrime and cyber warfare has prompted governments and international organizations to develop new legal frameworks to address these threats. However, the borderless nature of the internet and the anonymity it provides make it challenging to apply traditional legal concepts to the digital world.

One of the key challenges is jurisdiction. Cybercrimes often involve actors from different countries, making it difficult to determine which country's laws apply and how to prosecute offenders. International cooperation is essential for combating cybercrime, but differing legal systems, priorities, and levels of enforcement can complicate efforts to bring criminals to justice.

The United Nations and other international bodies have been working to establish norms and agreements for state behavior in cyberspace, particularly in the context of cyber warfare. However, reaching a consensus on what constitutes acceptable conduct and how to enforce these norms has proven difficult, as different countries have different views on issues such as state sovereignty, the use of force, and human rights in cyberspace.

The Role of Ethics in Technology Development: As technology continues to advance, there is a growing recognition of the need for ethical considerations to be integrated into the development and deployment of new technologies. This includes ensuring that technologies are designed and used in ways that respect privacy, promote fairness, and minimize harm.

The field of "tech ethics" has emerged in response to

these challenges, bringing together technologists, ethicists, policymakers, and other stakeholders to address the ethical implications of technology. This includes developing guidelines for ethical AI, ensuring transparency and accountability in data usage, and promoting the responsible development of new technologies.

However, the rapid pace of technological change often outstrips the ability of laws and ethical frameworks to keep up. As a result, there is a need for ongoing dialogue and collaboration between the tech industry, governments, and civil society to ensure that the benefits of technology are realized while mitigating the risks.

Conclusion

The internet has brought about unprecedented opportunities for communication, innovation, and global connectivity. However, it has also given rise to significant challenges, including the proliferation of cybercrime, the erosion of privacy, and the development of the dark web. These issues highlight the need for robust security measures, ethical considerations, and legal frameworks to navigate the complex digital landscape.

As we move further into the digital age, it is clear that the dark side of the internet will continue to pose significant challenges to individuals, businesses, and governments. Addressing these challenges requires a multifaceted approach that balances security with privacy, promotes ethical technology development, and fosters international cooperation to combat cyber threats.

The future of the internet will depend on our ability to navigate these challenges while harnessing the potential of technology to create a more secure, equitable, and connected world. The dark side of the internet serves as a reminder of the complexities and responsibilities that come with our increasingly digital lives, and the need for vigilance, innovation, and ethical considerations in shaping the future of the internet.

CHAPTER 17: THE EVOLUTION OF SEARCH ENGINES

Overview

This chapter explores the evolution of search engines, tracing their development from early pioneers like Alta Vista to the market dominance of Google. We will examine the technological advancements in search algorithms, the rise of Google and its transformative impact on the search engine market, the business models that have driven the success of search engines, including advertising, and the future trends in search technology.

The Technological Advancements in Search Algorithms

Early Search Engines: The origins of search engines can be traced back to the early 1990s when the World Wide Web was still in its infancy. As the web grew, so did the need for tools to help users find information amidst the rapidly expanding number of websites. Early search engines like Archie (1990) and Gopher (1991) were among the first attempts to index and search the internet, but they were limited in scope and functionality, focusing primarily on indexing file names and directories rather than the content within web pages.

One of the first true web search engines was **Alta Vista**, launched in 1995 by researchers at Digital Equipment

Corporation (DEC). Alta Vista was revolutionary for its time, offering the first full-text search of the web. Unlike its predecessors, which relied on human-edited directories or simple keyword matching, Alta Vista used automated web crawlers to index the entire content of web pages, making it possible to search for specific terms and phrases within documents. Alta Vista also introduced the concept of natural language queries, allowing users to search in everyday language rather than using complex Boolean operators.

The Development of Search Algorithms: As the volume of information on the web grew, so did the need for more sophisticated search algorithms. Early search engines like Alta Vista, Lycos, and Infoseek relied on relatively simple algorithms that ranked search results based on keyword frequency and meta tags. However, these methods were easily manipulated by webmasters using techniques like keyword stuffing, leading to irrelevant or low-quality search results.

The next major advancement in search technology came with the introduction of algorithms that considered the relationships between web pages. **PageRank,** developed by Larry Page and Sergey Brin at Stanford University in 1996, was a groundbreaking algorithm that transformed the search engine landscape. PageRank was based on the idea that the importance of a web page could be determined by the number and quality of links pointing to it. Pages with more inbound links from authoritative sources were considered more valuable and were ranked higher in search results.

PageRank represented a significant shift in search engine technology, as it moved beyond simple keyword matching to consider the broader context of the web. By analyzing the link structure of the internet, PageRank helped to surface more relevant and authoritative content, improving the overall quality of search results. This algorithm became the foundation of Google, which would soon become the dominant force in the search engine market.

The Evolution of Search Algorithms: As search engines continued to evolve, so did their algorithms. Google, in particular, has continually refined and expanded its search algorithms to deliver more accurate and useful results. In addition to PageRank, Google introduced algorithms that considered factors such as user behavior, content freshness, and semantic understanding.

One of the key developments in search technology has been the shift towards **semantic search.** Traditional search engines relied heavily on keyword matching, which often led to results that were technically relevant but did not fully capture the intent behind the user's query. Semantic search aims to understand the meaning and context of a query, allowing search engines to deliver results that are more aligned with what the user is actually looking for.

Google's **Hummingbird** update in 2013 was a significant step towards semantic search. Hummingbird focused on understanding the relationships between words and phrases in a query, enabling the search engine to provide better answers to complex or conversational queries. This was further enhanced by the introduction of **RankBrain** in 2015, an AI-driven algorithm that uses machine learning to interpret search queries and improve the relevance of search results.

The Rise of Personalized Search: Another major advancement in search technology has been the rise of personalized search. Search engines like Google now consider a wide range of factors to tailor search results to individual users, including their search history, location, and device. Personalized search aims to deliver more relevant and timely results by understanding the unique preferences and needs of each user.

While personalized search has improved the user experience by making search results more relevant, it has also raised concerns about the creation of "filter bubbles," where users are only exposed to information that aligns with their existing beliefs and interests. This has led to ongoing debates about the balance between personalization and diversity of information in search results.

The Rise of Google and Its Impact on the Search Engine Market

The Birth of Google: Google was founded in 1998 by Larry Page and Sergey Brin, two Stanford University Ph.D. students who developed the PageRank algorithm. Google started as a research project, but its potential was quickly recognized as it provided more relevant and accurate search results than any other search engine at the time. The minimalist design of Google's homepage, with its simple search box and lack of clutter, also set it apart from competitors that had evolved into portals filled with ads, news, and other distractions.

Google's search engine rapidly gained popularity, and by the early 2000s, it had overtaken established players like Alta Vista, Yahoo!, and Lycos to become the most widely used search engine in the world. Google's success was driven by its superior search results, user-friendly interface, and relentless focus on innovation.

Google's Impact on the Search Engine Market: The rise of Google had a profound impact on the search engine market, reshaping the industry and setting new standards for search technology. Google's dominance in search has led to a consolidation of the market, with many early competitors either exiting the industry or being acquired by other companies. Yahoo!, once a dominant force in search, shifted its focus to other areas, while Alta Vista was eventually shut down after being acquired by Yahoo!.

Google's dominance also influenced the way businesses approached online marketing and SEO (Search Engine Optimization). As Google became the primary gateway to the web, businesses realized the importance of appearing at the top of search results. This led to the growth of the SEO industry, with companies investing in optimizing their websites to rank higher on Google. The evolution of Google's algorithms has continually shaped SEO practices, as businesses adapt to new ranking factors and search trends.

The Expansion of Google's Services: While Google started as a search engine, the company quickly expanded into other areas, building an ecosystem of products and services that complemented its search engine. In 2000, Google launched **AdWords,** an advertising platform that allowed businesses to bid on keywords and have their ads displayed alongside search results. AdWords revolutionized online advertising, providing Google with a lucrative revenue stream and establishing search advertising as a key component of digital marketing.

Google also introduced services like **Gmail, Google Maps, Google News,** and **Google Images,** each of which became highly popular in their respective domains. The company's ability to integrate these services with its search engine further solidified its dominance, as users increasingly relied on Google for a wide range of online activities.

Google's Global Influence: Google's influence extends far beyond search, as the company has become a central player in the global digital economy. Google's Android operating system powers the majority of the world's smartphones, while its Chrome browser is the most widely used web browser globally. The company's search engine is available in hundreds of languages, and its services are used by billions of people around the world.

However, Google's dominance has also attracted scrutiny and criticism. The company has faced numerous antitrust investigations and legal challenges, particularly in Europe, where regulators have accused Google of using its market power to stifle competition. In 2018, the European Union fined Google €4.34 billion for antitrust violations related to its Android operating system, marking one of the largest fines ever imposed on a tech company.

Despite these challenges, Google remains the undisputed leader in the search engine market, with a market share of over 90% in most regions. The company's ability to innovate and adapt has allowed it to maintain its dominance in an ever-changing digital landscape.

The Business Models of Search Engines, Including Advertising

The Role of Advertising in Search Engines: Advertising has been the primary business model for search engines since the early 2000s. The ability to deliver highly targeted ads based on user search queries has made search engines one of the most effective and profitable advertising platforms in the digital age.

Google's AdWords, now known as **Google Ads,** is the most successful example of this model. Advertisers bid on keywords relevant to their business, and their ads are displayed alongside organic search results when users search for those keywords. Advertisers only pay when users click on their ads, a model known as pay-per-click (PPC) advertising. This performance-based model has proven highly effective, as it allows advertisers to reach potential customers at the moment they are actively searching for products or services.

The success of Google's advertising model has led other search engines, such as Bing and Yahoo!, to adopt similar approaches. The revenue generated from search advertising has allowed search engines to offer their services for free to users while investing in continuous improvements and innovations.

The Evolution of Search Advertising: Search advertising has evolved significantly since its inception. Early search ads were simple text-based links, but today's ads are more sophisticated, incorporating features like images, product listings, and extensions that provide additional information such as phone numbers, locations, and links to specific pages.

The introduction of **Google Shopping** ads, for example, allows retailers to display product images, prices, and availability directly in search results. This has made search ads more visually appealing and informative, driving higher engagement and conversion rates.

Another key development in search advertising has been the rise of **programmatic advertising,** which uses automated **systems and algorithms to buy and place ads in real-time.** Programmatic advertising leverages vast amounts of data to target specific audiences with personalized ads, making the advertising process more efficient and effective. In the context of search engines, programmatic systems help optimize ad placements based on factors such as user behavior, device type, location, and search history, ensuring that ads are shown to the most relevant users at the right time.

Google's **Smart Bidding** is an example of how machine learning and automation are being applied to search advertising. Smart Bidding automatically adjusts bids in real-time to maximize the chances of achieving specific goals, such as increasing website traffic, boosting sales, or enhancing return on investment (ROI). These advancements have made search advertising more accessible to businesses of all sizes, allowing even small companies to compete in the digital advertising space.

Alternative Revenue Models: While advertising remains the primary revenue model for search engines, some platforms have experimented with alternative approaches. For example, some search engines offer premium services or subscription models that provide enhanced features or an ad-free experience. **DuckDuckGo,** a privacy-focused search engine, generates revenue through affiliate marketing, where it earns a commission when users purchase products after clicking on links in its search results. This model allows DuckDuckGo to maintain a strong commitment to user privacy by not tracking or profiling users.

Another emerging trend is the integration of e-commerce directly into search engines. **Amazon,** while primarily an e-commerce platform, has effectively become a search engine for products, with millions of users starting their shopping journeys on the site. Amazon's search functionality is optimized to showcase relevant products, often including sponsored listings that generate additional revenue. This model blurs the line between search engines and e-commerce platforms, offering users a seamless experience from search to purchase.

The Role of Data in Monetization: The vast amounts of data generated by search engines are invaluable for monetization. Search engines collect data on user behavior, preferences, and demographics, which can be used to improve search results, target ads more effectively, and personalize the user experience. This data is also a valuable asset for market research, as it provides insights into consumer trends and behavior.

However, the use of data for monetization raises important ethical and privacy concerns. Users are increasingly aware of how their data is being collected and used, leading to growing demand for transparency and control over personal information. This has prompted search engines and regulators to implement stricter data protection measures, such as the European Union's General Data Protection Regulation (GDPR), which requires companies to obtain explicit consent before collecting personal data and to provide users with the ability to access and delete their data.

Future Trends in Search Technology

The Rise of Voice Search: Voice search is one of the most significant emerging trends in search technology. With the proliferation of voice-activated assistants like **Amazon Alexa, Google Assistant,** and **Apple Siri,** more users are turning to voice search as a convenient way to find information. Voice search is expected to account for a significant portion of all searches in the coming years, particularly on mobile devices and smart speakers.

Voice search presents new challenges and opportunities for search engines. Unlike traditional text-based searches, voice queries tend to be more conversational and often seek specific answers rather than a list of links. This has led to the development of more advanced natural language processing

(NLP) algorithms that can understand the intent behind voice queries and deliver more precise results.

For businesses, the rise of voice search requires a shift in SEO strategies. Optimizing for voice search involves focusing on natural language, question-based queries, and ensuring that information is easily accessible to voice assistants. As voice search continues to grow, it is likely to drive further innovation in search algorithms and user interfaces.

The Integration of AI and Machine Learning: Artificial intelligence (AI) and machine learning are playing an increasingly important role in the evolution of search engines. These technologies enable search engines to better understand and anticipate user intent, deliver more personalized results, and continuously improve through data-driven learning.

Google's **RankBrain** is a prime example of how AI is being integrated into search algorithms. RankBrain uses machine learning to interpret complex queries and understand the relationships between words and concepts. This allows Google to deliver more accurate and relevant results, even for queries it has never seen before. As AI continues to advance, we can expect search engines to become even more intuitive and capable of handling a wider range of queries.

AI is also being used to enhance image and video search capabilities. Traditional search engines rely on text-based metadata to index and retrieve images and videos, but AI-driven technologies like **computer vision** allow search engines to analyze the actual content of multimedia files. This enables more accurate and comprehensive search results, especially for users looking for specific visual content.

The Future of Search Interfaces: The way users interact with search engines is also evolving. Beyond voice search, we are seeing the rise of **visual search** and **augmented reality (AR)** as new interfaces for finding information. Visual search allows users to search the web using images instead of text. For example, Google Lens lets users take a photo of an object, landmark, or text, and receive relevant information, such as product details, historical facts, or translations.

AR is further blurring the lines between the digital and physical worlds, offering immersive search experiences. For example, AR-enabled search can allow users to point their smartphone camera at a product or location and receive real-time information overlaid on the physical environment. This technology has exciting applications in retail, tourism, education, and more.

Privacy-Focused Search Engines: As concerns about privacy continue to grow, there is increasing demand for search engines that prioritize user privacy and data protection. Search engines like **DuckDuckGo** and **Startpage** have gained popularity by offering anonymous search services that do not track users or store personal information.

Privacy-focused search engines are likely to continue gaining traction, especially as more users become aware of how their data is being used by traditional search engines. This trend could lead to a more diverse search engine market, with different players catering to different user preferences regarding privacy and data usage.

Search Beyond the Web: The concept of search is also expanding beyond the traditional web. As the Internet of Things (IoT) continues to grow, search engines are increasingly being integrated into connected devices, from smart home appliances to wearable technology. This evolution means that search will become more ubiquitous and embedded in our daily lives, allowing us to find information seamlessly across a wide range of contexts.

The future of search may also involve greater integration with other emerging technologies, such as blockchain and decentralized web (Web 3.0). These technologies could enable new forms of search that are more secure, transparent, and user-centric, potentially challenging the dominance of centralized search engines like Google.

Conclusion

The evolution of search engines has been one of the most remarkable stories in the history of the internet. From the early days of Alta Vista and basic keyword searches to the sophisticated, AI-driven platforms of today, search engines have continually adapted to the changing needs of users and the vast expansion of the web.

Google's rise to dominance reshaped the search engine market, setting new standards for relevance, speed, and user experience. The company's relentless focus on innovation, combined with its powerful advertising model, has allowed it to maintain its position as the leader in search technology for over two decades.

As we look to the future, search engines are poised to undergo further transformation, driven by advancements in AI, voice and visual search, and the growing importance of privacy. The way we search for information is evolving, and the next generation of search technology promises to be even more integrated, intuitive, and personalized.

The ongoing evolution of search engines will continue to shape how we access and interact with information in the digital age, influencing everything from business and commerce to education and entertainment. As search technology advances, it will remain a crucial tool in navigating the ever-expanding landscape of the internet.

CHAPTER 18: THE MOBILE INTERNET REVOLUTION

Overview

This chapter delves into the transformative impact of the mobile internet revolution, examining how the development of mobile networks and smartphones has reshaped online access and consumer behavior. We will explore the rise of mobile apps, the importance of responsive web design, and the profound changes in how people interact with the internet through mobile devices. Finally, we will look ahead to the future of mobile internet, considering emerging technologies that promise to further revolutionize the digital landscape.

The Development of Mobile Networks and Smartphones

The Evolution of Mobile Networks: The rise of mobile internet is closely linked to the development of mobile networks, which have evolved significantly over the past few decades. The journey began with the first-generation (1G) analog networks in the 1980s, which provided basic voice communication. The introduction of second-generation (2G) digital networks in the early 1990s marked a significant leap, enabling text messaging (SMS) and limited data services.

The true potential of mobile internet began to emerge with the rollout of third-generation (3G) networks in the early 2000s.

3G networks provided faster data transfer rates, allowing users to access the internet, send emails, and download multimedia content on their mobile devices. This was a turning point, as it enabled mobile devices to evolve from simple communication tools into multifunctional gadgets capable of accessing the web.

The advent of fourth-generation (4G) networks in the late 2000s and early 2010s took mobile internet to new heights. 4G networks offered significantly higher data speeds, low latency, and improved network reliability, making it possible to stream high-definition video, play online games, and use data-intensive applications on mobile devices. The widespread adoption of 4G was a key driver of the mobile internet revolution, enabling seamless, always-on connectivity.

The Birth of Smartphones: The development of smartphones was a critical factor in the rise of mobile internet. While early mobile phones were primarily designed for voice communication and text messaging, the introduction of smartphones transformed them into powerful computing devices capable of running a wide range of applications.

One of the first devices to popularize the concept of a smartphone was the **BlackBerry,** which gained popularity in the early 2000s, particularly among business users. BlackBerry devices featured a physical keyboard and were known for their robust email capabilities, making them a favorite tool for professionals who needed to stay connected on the go.

The true turning point in the smartphone era came with the launch of the **Apple iPhone** in 2007. The iPhone revolutionized the mobile phone industry with its innovative touch-screen interface, integrated multimedia features, and a user-friendly operating system (iOS). The iPhone's success was further amplified by the introduction of the **App Store** in 2008, which allowed developers to create and distribute mobile applications (apps) to millions of users worldwide.

The iPhone's impact was quickly followed by the rise of **Android,** Google's open-source mobile operating system, which launched in 2008. Android's flexibility and wide adoption by multiple manufacturers, such as Samsung, HTC, and Motorola, helped it quickly become the dominant mobile platform globally. The competition between iOS and Android fueled rapid innovation in the smartphone market, leading to the development of increasingly powerful and feature-rich devices.

The Integration of Mobile Internet into Daily Life: With the widespread adoption of smartphones, the internet became an integral part of daily life. People could now access the web, communicate, and interact with digital content anytime and anywhere. The convenience and accessibility of mobile internet changed the way people consumed information, socialized, and conducted business, leading to the emergence of the "always connected" lifestyle.

Smartphones also democratized access to technology, bringing the internet to regions and populations that previously had limited or no access to the web. As mobile networks expanded and smartphone prices dropped, billions of people around the world gained their first access to the internet through a mobile device, contributing to the global growth of internet usage.

The Impact of Mobile Apps and Responsive Web Design

The Rise of Mobile Apps: One of the most significant outcomes of the mobile internet revolution has been the rise of mobile apps. Apps are specialized software programs designed to run on smartphones and tablets, providing users with a tailored experience for specific tasks, such as messaging, social networking, gaming, shopping, and more.

The App Store and Google Play, the two largest app marketplaces, have become central to the mobile ecosystem, offering millions of apps across various categories. The availability of apps has greatly enhanced the functionality of smartphones, turning them into versatile tools that cater to virtually every aspect of modern life.

Mobile apps have also revolutionized industries by creating

new business models and revenue streams. For example, apps like **Uber** and **Lyft** transformed the transportation industry by enabling ride-hailing services through a simple tap on a smartphone. **Instagram** and **Snapchat** revolutionized social media by focusing on visual content and instant sharing. **WhatsApp** and **WeChat** reshaped global communication by providing free, instant messaging services that bypass traditional SMS.

For businesses, mobile apps have become essential for engaging with customers, providing services, and driving sales. Companies across industries have invested in developing their own apps to enhance customer experiences, streamline operations, and tap into the growing mobile market.

The Importance of Responsive Web Design: As mobile internet usage surged, it became clear that websites needed to adapt to the smaller screens and touch-based interfaces of smartphones and tablets. This led to the development of **responsive web design**, a design approach that ensures websites provide an optimal viewing experience across a wide range of devices and screen sizes.

Responsive web design uses flexible layouts, fluid grids, and CSS media queries to automatically adjust the appearance of a website based on the user's device. This ensures that content is easily readable, navigation is intuitive, and the overall user experience is seamless, whether the website is being viewed on a desktop computer, a tablet, or a smartphone.

The adoption of responsive web design became crucial for businesses as mobile internet traffic began to overtake desktop traffic. Websites that were not optimized for mobile devices risked losing visitors and potential customers due to poor user experiences. Google also began prioritizing mobile-friendly websites in its search rankings, further incentivizing businesses to adopt responsive design.

In addition to responsive design, the development of **Progressive Web Apps (PWAs)** provided an alternative to native apps by offering a mobile app-like experience directly through a web browser. PWAs combine the best features of both websites and apps, such as fast loading times, offline functionality, and push notifications, making them an attractive option for businesses looking to engage mobile users without the need for a dedicated app.

The Role of Mobile Commerce (mCommerce): The rise of mobile internet and apps has also driven the growth of **mobile commerce (mCommerce),** which refers to online shopping conducted via mobile devices. mCommerce has become a significant component of the e-commerce industry, with consumers increasingly using their smartphones to browse products, compare prices, and make purchases.

Retailers have responded by optimizing their websites and apps for mobile shopping, offering features like mobile wallets, one-click purchasing, and personalized recommendations. Mobile payment systems, such as **Apple Pay, Google Pay,** and **Samsung Pay,** have further facilitated the growth of mCommerce by providing secure, convenient payment options for mobile users.

The convenience of mCommerce has transformed consumer behavior, with many people now preferring to shop on their mobile devices rather than on desktops or in physical stores. The rise of mobile-first e-commerce platforms, such as **Wish** and **AliExpress,** has also contributed to the shift towards mobile shopping, particularly among younger consumers.

How Mobile Internet Has Changed Consumer Behavior

The Shift to Mobile-First Experiences: As smartphones became the primary means of accessing the internet, businesses and content creators began adopting a **mobile-first** approach, designing experiences specifically for mobile devices before adapting them for desktops. This shift was driven by the realization that the majority of online interactions were now taking place on mobile devices, making it essential to prioritize mobile users.

Mobile-first experiences focus on simplicity, speed, and ease of use, ensuring that users can quickly access the information or services they need with minimal effort. This approach has influenced everything from website design and app development to content creation and marketing strategies.

For example, social media platforms like Instagram and TikTok were designed from the ground up as mobile-first experiences, with features and interfaces optimized for vertical scrolling, touch gestures, and short attention spans. These platforms have redefined how people consume content, favoring quick, visual, and interactive formats that are well-suited to the mobile environment.

The Rise of Mobile Social Media: Mobile internet has also had a profound impact on social media usage. The convenience of accessing social media on the go has led to an increase in the frequency and duration of social media interactions. People are now more likely to check their social media accounts multiple times throughout the day, using their smartphones to stay connected with friends, family, and the latest trends.

The rise of mobile social media has also changed the way content is created and shared. Platforms like Instagram, Snapchat, and TikTok have popularized short-form, visually-driven content that can be easily consumed and shared on mobile devices. This has led to the emergence of new content formats, such as Stories and Reels, which are designed specifically for mobile viewing.

For marketers, the shift to mobile social media has created new opportunities to reach and engage with audiences. Mobile advertising, influencer marketing, and social commerce have become key components of digital marketing strategies, with brands leveraging the power of mobile social media to build relationships with consumers and drive sales.

The Impact on Consumer Expectations: The mobile internet revolution has raised consumer expectations for speed, convenience, and personalization. Mobile users expect websites and apps to load quickly, provide intuitive navigation, and deliver relevant content and recommendations based on their preferences , **behaviors, and location.** The "always connected" nature of smartphones means that consumers have become accustomed to accessing information and services instantly, leading to higher expectations for responsiveness and user experience across all digital platforms.

This shift has pushed businesses to innovate continuously, ensuring that their mobile offerings are not only functional but also optimized for speed and ease of use. Companies that fail to meet these expectations risk losing customers to competitors who can provide a better mobile experience.

Personalization and Mobile Commerce: The rise of mobile internet has also led to a demand for more personalized experiences. Consumers now expect brands to understand their preferences and deliver tailored content, offers, and recommendations. This has led to the widespread use of data analytics, artificial intelligence, and machine learning to create highly personalized mobile experiences.

In mobile commerce (mCommerce), personalization has become a key driver of sales. Retailers use data from past purchases, browsing history, and user profiles to recommend products that are likely to appeal to individual customers. Push notifications and personalized offers delivered through mobile apps and messaging platforms have become powerful tools for driving engagement and conversions.

Moreover, the convenience of mobile payment systems has facilitated the growth of impulse buying, as users can make purchases quickly and easily with just a few taps on their smartphones. The integration of one-click purchasing and mobile wallets has made the checkout process faster and more seamless, reducing cart abandonment rates and increasing sales.

The Influence of Mobile on Media Consumption: Mobile

internet has dramatically changed the way people consume media. The portability and convenience of smartphones have made them the preferred devices for consuming a wide range of content, from news and social media to music and video streaming.

The rise of streaming services like Netflix, Spotify, and YouTube has been closely linked to the proliferation of mobile devices. These platforms have optimized their apps for mobile use, allowing users to watch movies, listen to music, and consume video content on the go. The ability to download content for offline viewing has further enhanced the appeal of mobile streaming, enabling users to access their favorite media even when they are not connected to the internet.

Short-form content, in particular, has become increasingly popular on mobile devices. Platforms like TikTok, Instagram Reels, and Snapchat have capitalized on the trend of bite-sized videos, which are easy to consume in quick bursts throughout the day. This shift toward shorter, more visual content has influenced how media is produced and distributed, with traditional media companies and content creators adapting their strategies to meet the demands of mobile audiences.

Mobile-Driven Social Change: The mobile internet revolution has also played a significant role in driving social change. Mobile devices have empowered individuals and communities by providing them with tools to communicate, organize, and advocate for their rights. Social movements like the Arab Spring, Black Lives Matter, and #MeToo have been amplified by mobile internet, as activists use smartphones to document events, share information, and mobilize supporters.

In many developing countries, mobile phones have become the primary means of accessing the internet, enabling people to participate in the global digital economy and connect with others beyond their immediate communities. Mobile internet has facilitated access to education, healthcare, and financial services, helping to bridge the digital divide and improve quality of life for millions of people around the world.

However, the widespread use of mobile internet has also raised concerns about privacy, data security, and the potential for digital surveillance. The ease with which mobile devices can be tracked and monitored has led to debates about the balance between convenience and the protection of personal freedoms in the digital age.

The Future of Mobile Internet and Emerging Technologies

The Rollout of 5G Networks: One of the most significant developments in the future of mobile internet is the rollout of fifth-generation (5G) networks. 5G promises to deliver faster data speeds, lower latency, and greater network capacity compared to 4G, enabling a new era of connected devices and immersive experiences.

The enhanced capabilities of 5G will pave the way for innovations such as augmented reality (AR), virtual reality (VR), and the Internet of Things (IoT). With 5G, users will be able to stream high-definition content, participate in real-time online gaming, and interact with smart devices more seamlessly than ever before. The increased bandwidth and reliability of 5G networks will also support the growth of smart cities, autonomous vehicles, and other emerging technologies that rely on constant, high-speed connectivity.

For businesses, 5G will open up new opportunities for innovation and efficiency. Industries such as healthcare, manufacturing, and logistics will benefit from the ability to deploy IoT devices and sensors that can communicate in real-time, enabling smarter decision-making and automation. The potential for 5G to revolutionize industries and improve everyday life makes it one of the most anticipated advancements in mobile internet.

The Integration of AI and Machine Learning: Artificial intelligence (AI) and machine learning will continue to play a crucial role in the evolution of mobile internet. These technologies are already being used to enhance mobile experiences through personalization, predictive analytics, and intelligent assistants like Siri, Google Assistant, and Alexa.

In the future, AI-driven mobile apps will become even more sophisticated, capable of anticipating user needs and delivering highly personalized content and services. Machine learning algorithms will enable apps to learn from user behavior and adapt in real-time, providing more relevant recommendations and improving overall user engagement.

AI will also drive advancements in mobile security, with predictive models capable of detecting and mitigating threats before they can cause harm. This will be particularly important as mobile devices continue to be central to personal and professional life, making them attractive targets for cybercriminals.

The Expansion of Augmented and Virtual Reality: Augmented reality (AR) and virtual reality (VR) are poised to become integral parts of the mobile internet experience. AR, which overlays digital information onto the real world, has already gained traction through apps like Pokémon GO and Snapchat filters. As mobile devices become more powerful and 5G networks roll out, AR experiences will become more immersive and widespread, transforming industries such as retail, education, and entertainment.

Virtual reality, while currently more limited by hardware constraints, is also expected to benefit from advancements in mobile technology. Future smartphones may be capable of delivering high-quality VR experiences without the need for external headsets, making VR more accessible to mainstream consumers. The combination of AR and VR, often referred to as mixed reality, will create new possibilities for interactive and immersive content, from virtual shopping experiences to remote collaboration in virtual workspaces.

Wearable Technology and the Internet of Things: Wearable technology and the Internet of Things (IoT) are closely linked to the future of mobile internet. Devices such as smartwatches, fitness trackers, and connected home appliances are becoming increasingly common, with many of them relying on mobile internet to function effectively.

The integration of IoT devices with mobile networks will enable smarter, more connected environments, where everyday objects can communicate with each other and respond to user commands. This will lead to greater convenience, efficiency, and automation in areas such as home management, healthcare, and transportation.

Wearable technology will also continue to evolve, with new devices offering more advanced health monitoring, communication, and productivity features. As these devices become more capable, they will further integrate with the mobile ecosystem, providing users with seamless access to information and services wherever they go.

Privacy and Security Challenges: As mobile internet continues to evolve, privacy and security will remain critical concerns. The increasing amount of personal data stored on mobile devices, combined with the growing connectivity of IoT devices, creates new vulnerabilities that cybercriminals can exploit. Ensuring the security of mobile networks, apps, and devices will require ongoing innovation and collaboration between tech companies, regulators, and security experts.

Privacy concerns will also need to be addressed, particularly as AI-driven personalization and data collection become more pervasive. Consumers are becoming more aware of how their data is being used, leading to greater demand for transparency, control, and data protection. The future of mobile internet will likely see the development of new privacy-enhancing technologies and regulations aimed at protecting users' rights while enabling the benefits of a connected world.

Conclusion

The mobile internet revolution has fundamentally transformed how we access and interact with the digital world. The development of mobile networks and smartphones has brought the internet into the hands of billions of people, changing consumer behavior, media consumption, and the global economy. The rise of mobile apps, responsive web design, and personalized experiences has reshaped industries and created new opportunities for innovation and growth.

As we look to the future, the continued evolution of mobile internet, driven by advancements in 5G, AI, AR, and IoT, promises to unlock even greater possibilities. However, these advancements will also bring new challenges, particularly in the areas of privacy, security, and ethical considerations. Navigating these challenges while harnessing the full potential of mobile technology will be key to shaping the future of the internet and ensuring that its benefits are accessible to all.

The mobile internet revolution is far from over, and its impact will continue to be felt across all aspects of society in the years to come. As we move forward, the ability to innovate, adapt, and address the challenges of a rapidly changing digital landscape will determine the future of mobile internet and its role in our increasingly connected world.

CHAPTER 19: THE CLOUD AND BEYOND

Overview

This chapter explores the development of cloud computing, a transformative technology that has reshaped internet infrastructure, data storage, and services. We will trace the origins and growth of cloud computing, examine how cloud services have revolutionized data storage and access, and analyze the impact of major players like Amazon Web Services (AWS) and Microsoft Azure. Finally, we will look ahead to the future of cloud computing, considering potential challenges and the technologies that may shape the next phase of its evolution.

The Origins and Growth of Cloud Computing

The Early Concepts of Cloud Computing: The concept of cloud computing can be traced back to the 1960s when computer scientist John McCarthy, who was instrumental in the development of time-sharing systems, predicted that computing would one day be organized as a public utility, much like electricity or water. However, the technology and infrastructure required to realize this vision did not exist at the time, and it would take several decades for the idea to become a reality.

The foundation of cloud computing began to take shape in the 1990s with the development of virtualization technology. Virtualization allows multiple virtual machines (VMs) to run on a single physical server, enabling more efficient use of computing resources. This technology laid the groundwork for cloud computing by making it possible to deliver computing resources as a service, rather than as a product.

In the early 2000s, the concept of cloud computing started to gain traction with the advent of web-based services. Companies like Salesforce.com pioneered the Software-as-a-Service (SaaS) model, where software applications were hosted on remote servers and accessed via the internet. This model provided businesses with the flexibility to use software without the need to install and maintain it on local machines, paving the way for broader adoption of cloud-based services.

The Emergence of Cloud Infrastructure: The true breakthrough in cloud computing came with the launch of Amazon Web Services (AWS) in 2006. AWS introduced the Infrastructure-as-a-Service (IaaS) model, which provided on-demand access to computing resources such as servers, storage, and databases over the internet. AWS's first service, Amazon Elastic Compute Cloud (EC2), allowed businesses to rent virtual servers on an as-needed basis, paying only for the resources they used.

The launch of AWS marked a turning point in the evolution of cloud computing, as it demonstrated the scalability, flexibility, and cost-effectiveness of cloud infrastructure. Businesses of all sizes could now access powerful computing resources without the need to invest in expensive hardware or manage complex IT infrastructure. This democratization of computing power led to rapid growth in cloud adoption, as companies recognized the potential of cloud computing to drive innovation and efficiency.

Following AWS's success, other major tech companies entered the cloud computing market. Google launched its cloud platform, Google Cloud, in 2008, and Microsoft introduced Azure in 2010. These platforms, along with AWS, quickly became the leading providers of cloud services, offering a wide range of products and solutions that catered to the diverse needs of businesses across industries.

The Evolution of Cloud Services: Cloud computing has

evolved significantly since its inception, with the introduction of new service models and capabilities. In addition to IaaS and SaaS, the Platform-as-a-Service (PaaS) model emerged, providing developers with a platform to build, deploy, and manage applications without having to worry about the underlying infrastructure. PaaS services include development tools, databases, and runtime environments, enabling faster and more efficient application development.

Another key development in cloud computing has been the rise of multi-cloud and hybrid cloud strategies. Many organizations now use a combination of public and private clouds, as well as multiple cloud providers, to meet their specific needs. Hybrid cloud environments allow businesses to take advantage of the scalability and cost-effectiveness of public clouds while maintaining control over sensitive data and workloads in private clouds.

The growth of cloud computing has also led to the emergence of specialized cloud services, such as Data-as-a-Service (DaaS), Artificial Intelligence-as-a-Service (AIaaS), and Machine Learning-as-a-Service (MLaaS). These services provide businesses with access to advanced technologies and data analytics capabilities, enabling them to harness the power of big data and AI without the need for in-house expertise.

How Cloud Services Have Changed Data Storage and Access

The Shift from On-Premises to Cloud Storage: Before the advent of cloud computing, businesses typically relied on on-premises data centers to store and manage their data. These data centers required significant investments in hardware, software, and maintenance, and were often limited in their ability to scale to meet growing demands. The move to cloud storage has fundamentally changed the way data is stored, managed, and accessed.

Cloud storage allows businesses to store data on remote servers maintained by cloud service providers, eliminating the need for on-premises infrastructure. This shift has several key advantages, including scalability, cost-efficiency, and accessibility. Cloud storage is highly scalable, allowing businesses to increase or decrease their storage capacity based on demand, without the need for upfront investments in hardware. This pay-as-you-go model has made it easier for businesses to manage their storage costs and adapt to changing needs.

Cloud storage also provides enhanced accessibility, as data stored in the cloud can be accessed from anywhere with an internet connection. This has enabled greater collaboration and flexibility, particularly in the era of remote work, as employees can access files and applications from any device, regardless of their location. Additionally, cloud storage services often include built-in redundancy and disaster recovery features, ensuring that data is protected and available even in the event of hardware failures or other disruptions.

The Impact on Data Management and Analytics: The rise of cloud computing has also transformed the way businesses manage and analyze data. Cloud-based data management platforms, such as Amazon S3, Google Cloud Storage, and Microsoft Azure Blob Storage, provide businesses with powerful tools to organize, secure, and analyze large volumes of data.

One of the most significant developments in cloud data management has been the integration of big data and analytics capabilities. Cloud platforms offer a range of data processing and analytics services, such as Amazon Redshift, Google BigQuery, and Azure Synapse Analytics, which allow businesses to process and analyze massive datasets in real-time. These services enable organizations to gain valuable insights from their data, driving more informed decision-making and enhancing their ability to compete in a data-driven economy.

The cloud has also facilitated the adoption of artificial intelligence (AI) and machine learning (ML) technologies. Cloud-based AI and ML services, such as Google Cloud AI and Azure

Machine Learning, provide businesses with access to advanced algorithms and models that can be used to automate processes, predict outcomes, and personalize customer experiences. The ability to leverage AI and ML without the need for in-house expertise has democratized access to these technologies, enabling businesses of all sizes to harness the power of AI.

The Rise of Cloud-Native Applications: Cloud computing has given rise to a new generation of applications designed specifically for the cloud environment. These "cloud-native" applications are built to take full advantage of the scalability, flexibility, and resilience of cloud infrastructure. Unlike traditional applications that are simply migrated to the cloud, cloud-native applications are designed from the ground up to operate in a distributed and dynamic environment.

Key features of cloud-native applications include microservices architecture, containerization, and continuous integration/continuous deployment (CI/CD) pipelines. Microservices architecture allows applications to be broken down into smaller, independent components that can be developed, deployed, and scaled independently. Containerization, using tools like Docker and Kubernetes, enables these microservices to be packaged and run consistently across different environments. CI/CD pipelines automate the process of building, testing, and deploying applications, enabling faster and more reliable updates.

Cloud-native applications have become the standard for modern software development, enabling businesses to innovate more rapidly and respond to changing market demands. The ability to deploy and scale applications quickly and efficiently has become a key competitive advantage in the digital economy.

The Role of Major Players Like Amazon Web Services and Microsoft Azure

Amazon Web Services (AWS): Amazon Web Services (AWS) is widely regarded as the pioneer and leader in the cloud computing industry. Since its launch in 2006, AWS has grown into the largest and most comprehensive cloud platform, offering a vast array of services across computing, storage, databases, networking, analytics, machine learning, security, and more.

AWS's success can be attributed to its early entry into the market, its relentless focus on innovation, and its customer-centric approach. AWS was the first to introduce the IaaS model, allowing businesses to rent virtual servers and storage on-demand. Over the years, AWS has continued to expand its offerings, introducing new services and features that cater to the evolving needs of its customers.

One of the key strengths of AWS is its global infrastructure, with data centers (referred to as "regions") located around the world. This global reach allows AWS to provide low-latency access to its services, as well as robust redundancy and disaster recovery options. AWS's scale and reliability have made it the platform of choice for many of the world's largest enterprises, as well as startups and government agencies.

AWS's dominance in the cloud market has also made it a significant contributor to Amazon's overall revenue and profitability. The success of AWS has enabled Amazon to invest in new technologies and services, further solidifying its position as a leader in the cloud industry.

Microsoft Azure: Microsoft Azure, launched in 2010, is another major player in the cloud computing market. Azure has quickly become the second-largest cloud platform, offering a broad range of services that compete directly with AWS. Azure's success is largely due to Microsoft's deep enterprise relationships, its extensive product portfolio, and its focus on hybrid cloud solutions.

One of Azure's key differentiators is its strong integration with Microsoft's existing software and services, such as Windows Server, Active Directory, and Office 365. This integration has made Azure an attractive option for businesses that rely on Microsoft **technologies,** as it provides a seamless environment for extending their on-premises infrastructure to the cloud. Azure's hybrid cloud capabilities, which allow businesses to run applications and manage workloads across both on-premises data centers and the cloud, have been particularly appealing to organizations that need to maintain a balance between cloud and on-premises resources.

Azure has also been a leader in supporting open-source technologies and multi-cloud strategies. The platform offers extensive support for Linux, Kubernetes, and other open-source tools, allowing businesses to build and deploy applications using the technologies that best suit their needs. Additionally, Azure's commitment to interoperability and integration with other cloud providers has made it a key player in multi-cloud environments, where businesses use services from multiple cloud providers to optimize their operations.

Microsoft has leveraged its expertise in artificial intelligence (AI) and machine learning (ML) to differentiate Azure in the cloud market. Azure AI and Azure Machine Learning provide a comprehensive suite of tools and services for building, training, and deploying AI and ML models, making it easier for businesses to incorporate advanced analytics into their operations.

Azure's global network of data centers, along with its investments in security, compliance, and regulatory support, have made it a trusted platform for enterprises and government agencies around the world. Microsoft's emphasis on security and privacy has been a key factor in Azure's adoption, particularly in industries with stringent regulatory requirements, such as finance, healthcare, and government.

Google Cloud: Google Cloud, while not as dominant as AWS or Azure, has established itself as a strong competitor in the cloud computing market. Google Cloud's strengths lie in its expertise in data analytics, artificial intelligence, and machine learning, which have made it the platform of choice for organizations seeking to leverage big data and AI capabilities.

Google Cloud's flagship services include BigQuery, a fully

managed, serverless data warehouse that enables fast and scalable analytics on large datasets, and TensorFlow, an open-source machine learning framework that has become a standard tool for AI development. Google Cloud's data and AI services have been widely adopted by businesses in industries such as retail, healthcare, and finance, where data-driven decision-making is critical.

Google's commitment to open-source technologies and multi-cloud strategies has also been a key factor in its growth. Google Kubernetes Engine (GKE) is one of the most popular managed Kubernetes services, enabling businesses to deploy, manage, and scale containerized applications in the cloud. Google's leadership in the development of Kubernetes, as well as its support for hybrid and multi-cloud deployments, has made it an attractive option for organizations looking to build flexible and scalable cloud environments.

While Google Cloud's market share is smaller than that of AWS and Azure, the platform has seen significant growth in recent years, driven by its investments in enterprise solutions, security, and global infrastructure. Google Cloud's focus on innovation and its ability to integrate cutting-edge technologies into its services have positioned it as a key player in the cloud computing market.

The Competitive Landscape: The cloud computing market is highly competitive, with AWS, Microsoft Azure, and Google Cloud vying for dominance. Each of these providers offers a unique set of strengths and capabilities, catering to different customer needs and preferences. While AWS remains the largest and most comprehensive cloud platform, Azure and Google Cloud have made significant inroads by focusing on hybrid cloud, AI, data analytics, and multi-cloud strategies.

In addition to these major players, there are several other cloud providers that offer specialized services or cater to specific markets. IBM Cloud, for example, is known for its focus on enterprise solutions, AI, and hybrid cloud, while Oracle Cloud is popular in the enterprise resource planning (ERP) and database markets. Alibaba Cloud, the leading cloud provider in China, has expanded its services globally, offering competitive solutions in e-commerce, finance, and AI.

The competition among cloud providers has driven rapid innovation, with each platform continuously introducing new services, features, and pricing models to attract customers. This competition has benefited businesses by providing them with a wide range of options and driving down the cost of cloud services.

The Future of Cloud Computing and Potential Challenges

Edge Computing and the Next Phase of Cloud Evolution: One of the most significant trends shaping the future of cloud computing is the rise of edge computing. Edge computing involves processing data closer to the source of data generation, such as IoT devices or local servers, rather than relying solely on centralized cloud data centers. This approach reduces latency, improves performance, and enables real-time processing of data, making it ideal for applications such as autonomous vehicles, smart cities, and industrial automation.

As more devices become connected and generate massive amounts of data, edge computing is expected to play a critical role in complementing cloud services. Major cloud providers are already investing in edge computing solutions, integrating edge capabilities with their cloud platforms to offer a more distributed computing environment. For example, AWS offers services like AWS IoT Greengrass and AWS Wavelength, which extend cloud capabilities to the edge, enabling low-latency processing for IoT and 5G applications.

The integration of edge computing with cloud services will create a more dynamic and flexible computing environment, allowing businesses to deploy applications and process data wherever it makes the most sense—whether in the cloud, at the edge, or a combination of both.

The Role of Artificial Intelligence and Automation: Artificial intelligence (AI) and automation will continue to play a central role in the future of cloud computing. Cloud providers are increasingly incorporating AI and machine learning capabilities into their platforms, enabling businesses to automate processes, optimize operations, and gain insights from data at scale.

AI-driven cloud services, such as intelligent automation, predictive analytics, and natural language processing, will become more accessible to businesses of all sizes, democratizing access to advanced technologies. The use of AI in cloud management will also improve the efficiency and reliability of cloud operations, with automated systems capable of optimizing resource allocation, detecting anomalies, and responding to incidents in real-time.

As AI becomes more integrated into cloud platforms, we can expect to see the development of more sophisticated AI-driven applications, from autonomous systems to personalized digital assistants. The combination of cloud computing and AI will unlock new possibilities for innovation, transforming industries and creating new business models.

The Challenges of Data Privacy and Security: As cloud computing continues to evolve, data privacy and security will remain critical challenges. The increasing volume of data stored and processed in the cloud, combined with the growing sophistication of cyber threats, has raised concerns about the security of cloud environments.

Cloud providers have made significant investments in security, offering advanced encryption, access control, and threat detection services to protect customer data. However, the shared responsibility model of cloud security, where both the cloud provider and the customer share responsibility for securing data, can create gaps in protection if not properly managed.

Data privacy regulations, such as the European Union's

General Data Protection Regulation (GDPR) and the California Consumer Privacy Act (CCPA), have added complexity to the cloud computing landscape, requiring businesses to comply with strict data protection requirements. As more countries introduce their own data privacy laws, cloud providers will need to navigate a patchwork of regulations, ensuring that their services are compliant across different jurisdictions.

The challenge of maintaining data sovereignty—ensuring that data remains within specific geographic boundaries—will also become more pronounced as businesses operate in an increasingly globalized world. Cloud providers will need to offer solutions that address these concerns, such as data localization and region-specific services, to meet the needs of customers with strict regulatory requirements.

Sustainability and the Environmental Impact of Cloud Computing: The rapid growth of cloud computing has raised concerns about its environmental impact. Data centers, which power cloud services, consume significant amounts of energy and generate substantial carbon emissions. As cloud adoption continues to grow, the industry faces increasing pressure to reduce its environmental footprint and adopt more sustainable practices.

Major cloud providers have made commitments to sustainability, investing in renewable energy, improving energy efficiency, and developing carbon-neutral data centers. For example, Google has been carbon-neutral since 2007 and aims to operate entirely on carbon-free energy by 2030. AWS and Microsoft have also set ambitious sustainability goals, including achieving net-zero carbon emissions and increasing the use of renewable energy in their operations.

The future of cloud computing will likely involve a greater focus on sustainability, with cloud providers working to minimize their environmental impact while meeting the growing demand for cloud services. Innovations in data center design, energy management, and cooling technologies will play a key role in achieving these goals, as will the adoption of more efficient computing architectures and practices.

The Potential of Quantum Computing: Quantum computing is an emerging technology that has the potential to revolutionize cloud computing by solving complex problems that are beyond the capabilities of classical computers. Quantum computers leverage the principles of quantum mechanics to perform calculations at speeds that are exponentially faster than traditional computers.

While quantum computing is still in its early stages, major cloud providers like AWS, Microsoft, and Google are investing in quantum research and offering early-stage quantum computing services through their cloud platforms. These services, such as Amazon Braket, Microsoft Azure Quantum, and Google Quantum AI, allow businesses and researchers to experiment with quantum algorithms and explore the potential applications of quantum computing.

The integration of quantum computing into cloud platforms could unlock new possibilities for fields such as cryptography, materials science, drug discovery, and artificial intelligence. However, the development of practical quantum computers is still years away, and significant challenges remain in terms of scalability, error correction, and the development of quantum algorithms.

Conclusion

Cloud computing has fundamentally transformed the internet, providing businesses and individuals with scalable, flexible, and cost-effective access to computing resources and services. The development of cloud infrastructure, led by major players like Amazon Web Services, Microsoft Azure, and Google Cloud, has enabled the rapid growth of digital innovation, from data analytics and artificial intelligence to mobile applications and remote work.

As cloud computing continues to evolve, new trends and

technologies, such as edge computing, AI, and quantum computing, will shape the future of the cloud landscape. However, this evolution also brings challenges, particularly in areas such as data privacy, security, sustainability, and **the ethical implications of advanced technologies.** The cloud's future will depend on the ability of providers, businesses, and governments to navigate these challenges while continuing to innovate and deliver value to users.

The continued growth of cloud computing will likely lead to even greater integration of cloud services into all aspects of society, from healthcare and education to finance and entertainment. As more industries embrace digital transformation, cloud computing will remain at the heart of this shift, enabling organizations to be more agile, data-driven, and customer-focused.

However, the cloud's impact goes beyond business and technology—it also raises important questions about the future of work, privacy, and the environment. The balance between the benefits of cloud computing and its potential downsides will be a key focus in the years to come. This includes addressing concerns about data sovereignty, the environmental footprint of data centers, and the ethical use of AI and automation in cloud-based applications.

Looking ahead, cloud computing will continue to be a driving force behind the most significant technological advancements of our time. From the rise of smart cities and autonomous vehicles to the potential of quantum computing and the next generation of AI, the cloud will serve as the backbone of these innovations, supporting the infrastructure, data processing, and analytics needed to bring them to life.

As we move further into the era of cloud computing and beyond, the lessons learned from its evolution will be crucial in guiding future developments in technology. The cloud has already reshaped the digital landscape in profound ways, and its influence will only grow as new challenges and opportunities emerge. By understanding the cloud's past and present, we can better prepare for the transformative changes that lie ahead, ensuring that the benefits of cloud computing are accessible, sustainable, and secure for everyone.

CHAPTER 20: THE INTERNET'S FUTURE: CHALLENGES AND OPPORTUNITIES

Overview

As we conclude this exploration of the internet's history and development, it is crucial to consider the road ahead. The future of the internet is shaped by emerging technologies, ongoing challenges, and the ever-evolving needs of society. In this chapter, we will delve into the potential of quantum computing and artificial intelligence (AI) to revolutionize the internet, discuss the challenges of maintaining net neutrality and open access, and examine the internet's role in shaping future societies. Finally, we will explore predictions from experts and visionaries about what lies ahead for the internet.

The Potential of Quantum Computing and AI in the Internet's Evolution

Quantum Computing: A New Frontier: Quantum computing represents one of the most exciting and potentially transformative advancements in technology, with profound implications for the future of the internet. Unlike classical computers, which use bits as the basic unit of information, quantum computers use quantum bits, or qubits, which can exist in multiple states simultaneously thanks to the principles of superposition and entanglement. This allows quantum computers to perform complex calculations at speeds exponentially faster than today's most powerful supercomputers.

The potential applications of quantum computing in the internet are vast. In cryptography, quantum computers could break existing encryption methods, leading to the need for new, quantum-resistant algorithms. On the other hand, quantum encryption could offer unprecedented levels of security, making data breaches virtually impossible. Quantum computing could also revolutionize data processing and analysis, enabling the rapid solution of problems that are currently intractable, such as simulating molecular interactions for drug discovery or optimizing global supply chains in real-time.

However, the integration of quantum computing into the internet will also present significant challenges. The development of practical, large-scale quantum computers is still in its early stages, and there are substantial technical hurdles to overcome, including error correction, qubit stability, and the creation of a quantum internet that can transmit qubits over long distances without decoherence.

Artificial Intelligence and the Future of the Internet: Artificial intelligence (AI) has already begun to reshape the internet, and its influence will only grow in the coming years. AI technologies, including machine learning, natural language processing, and computer vision, are being integrated into every aspect of the internet, from search engines and social media algorithms to cybersecurity and personalized content delivery.

One of the key areas where AI will impact the future of the internet is in automation. AI-driven automation will streamline many online processes, from customer service chatbots to automated content moderation on social media platforms. This will not only improve efficiency but also help manage the vast amounts of data generated by the internet, making it easier to extract meaningful insights and deliver personalized experiences to users.

AI will also play a crucial role in enhancing cybersecurity. As cyber threats become more sophisticated, AI-driven systems will be essential for detecting and responding to attacks in real-time. Machine learning algorithms can analyze patterns of behavior to identify anomalies that may indicate a security breach, while AI-powered tools can automate the process of patching vulnerabilities and mitigating threats.

The combination of AI and big data will enable more advanced predictive analytics, allowing businesses and governments to anticipate trends and make data-driven decisions. However, the widespread adoption of AI also raises ethical and societal concerns, such as the potential for bias in AI algorithms, the impact on employment, and the need for transparency and accountability in AI-driven decision-making.

As AI continues to evolve, it will become increasingly important to ensure that its development and deployment align with ethical principles and human values. This will require ongoing collaboration between technologists, policymakers, and civil society to address the challenges and opportunities presented by AI in the internet's future.

The Challenges of Maintaining Net Neutrality and Open Access

The Importance of Net Neutrality: Net neutrality is the principle that internet service providers (ISPs) should treat all data on the internet equally, without discriminating against or favoring particular websites, services, or applications. This principle has been fundamental to the open and democratic nature of the internet, ensuring that users have equal access to information and that innovation can thrive without undue interference.

However, net neutrality has been the subject of intense debate and legal battles in recent years. Proponents of net neutrality argue that without it, ISPs could create "fast lanes" for content providers who can afford to pay for better service, while relegating others to slower speeds. This could stifle competition, limit freedom of expression, and create a tiered internet where access to information is determined by economic power.

Opponents of net neutrality, on the other hand, argue that ISPs should have the flexibility to manage their networks as they see fit, including offering different levels of service based on pricing. They also contend that the market, rather than regulation, should determine how internet services are provided.

The challenge of maintaining net neutrality is likely to continue as governments around the world grapple with how to regulate the internet. In the United States, the Federal Communications Commission (FCC) has seen net neutrality rules implemented, repealed, and debated multiple times. In other countries, similar debates are ongoing, with varying outcomes depending on local regulatory environments.

The future of net neutrality will have significant implications for the internet's openness, accessibility, and innovation. As technology continues to advance and the demand for bandwidth-intensive services like streaming and gaming grows, the pressure on ISPs to manage network traffic will increase. How governments and regulators address these challenges will play a critical role in shaping the future of the internet.

Ensuring Open Access and Bridging the Digital Divide: Open access to the internet is a cornerstone of its potential to empower individuals, promote innovation, and foster economic growth. However, despite significant advancements in connectivity, the digital divide—the gap between those who have access to the internet and those who do not—remains a pressing issue.

In many parts of the world, particularly in rural and underserved communities, access to high-speed internet is limited or nonexistent. This digital divide exacerbates existing inequalities, limiting access to education, healthcare, and economic opportunities. As the internet becomes increasingly essential for participation in modern society, addressing this divide is critical.

Efforts to bridge the digital divide include government initiatives to expand broadband infrastructure, public-private partnerships to deliver affordable internet access, and innovative technologies such as satellite internet and community-based networks. For example, initiatives like SpaceX's Starlink aim to provide high-speed internet to remote and underserved areas through a network of low-Earth orbit satellites.

However, ensuring open access to the internet also involves addressing issues of affordability, digital literacy, and censorship. Even where internet infrastructure exists, high costs and a lack of digital skills can prevent people from fully benefiting from online resources. Additionally, in some countries, government censorship and restrictions on internet access limit the free flow of information, stifling freedom of expression and innovation.

The future of the internet depends on our ability to ensure that it remains open and accessible to all. This will require ongoing efforts to expand connectivity, promote digital literacy, and protect the internet from censorship and undue control by both governments and private entities.

The Role of the Internet in Shaping Future Societies

The Internet as a Driver of Social Change: The internet has already had a profound impact on society, serving as a platform for social movements, political activism, and cultural exchange. As we look to the future, the internet will continue to play a central role in shaping social, political, and economic dynamics.

Social media platforms, in particular, have become powerful tools for organizing and mobilizing communities around shared causes. Movements like #MeToo, Black Lives Matter, and climate activism have gained global momentum through the internet, highlighting its ability to amplify marginalized voices and bring attention to critical issues. The internet also enables cross-border collaboration, allowing people to connect, share knowledge, and work together on global challenges such as climate change, human rights, and public health.

However, the internet's influence on society is not without its challenges. The spread of misinformation, the rise of echo chambers, and the potential for online radicalization pose significant risks to social cohesion and democratic processes. The internet's role in shaping public opinion and influencing elections has become a major concern, with growing awareness of the need for transparency, accountability, and media literacy in the digital age.

As the internet continues to evolve, its impact on society will be shaped by how we address these challenges. Ensuring that the internet remains a force for positive social change will require a collective effort to promote digital literacy, combat misinformation, and foster inclusive and diverse online communities.

The Future of Work in a Connected World: The internet has transformed the way we work, enabling remote work, gig economy platforms, and global collaboration. The COVID-19 pandemic accelerated these trends, with remote work becoming the norm for many employees and businesses recognizing the benefits of flexible work arrangements.

As we move into the future, the internet will continue to shape the world of work, with emerging technologies like AI, automation, and the gig economy redefining traditional employment models. Remote work is likely to remain a significant aspect of the workforce, with businesses adopting hybrid models that combine in-person and remote work to maximize productivity and employee satisfaction.

The rise of the gig economy, facilitated by platforms like Uber, Upwork, and Fiverr, has created new opportunities for independent work, but it has also raised concerns about job security, worker rights, and income inequality. As more people engage in gig work, there will be a growing need for policies and protections that address the unique challenges faced by gig workers.

AI and automation will also have a profound impact on the future of work, with the potential to both create new opportunities and displace existing jobs. While AI can enhance productivity and innovation, it also raises questions about the future of employment and the need for reskilling and upskilling programs to prepare workers for the changing job market.

The internet's role in the future of work will be shaped by how we address these challenges and opportunities. As technology continues to evolve, there will be a need for policies and strategies that ensure **the benefits of these advancements are shared broadly across society while mitigating potential downsides.** This includes developing frameworks that protect workers' rights in the gig economy, ensuring equitable access to remote work opportunities, and investing in education and training programs to prepare the workforce for the jobs of the future.

The Internet and the Future of Governance: The internet has significantly impacted governance, enabling greater transparency, citizen engagement, and the potential for digital democracy. Governments worldwide are increasingly using digital platforms to provide public services, engage with citizens, and collect data for policymaking. The rise of e-governance, which leverages the internet to improve government efficiency and accessibility, has the potential to transform how citizens interact with their governments.

For example, digital platforms can streamline processes such as voting, tax filing, and accessing public services, making government more responsive and accessible. In some countries, initiatives like Estonia's e-Residency program have demonstrated the potential of digital governance to enhance global connectivity and economic inclusion by allowing people to start and run businesses in Estonia without physically residing there.

However, the digitization of governance also presents challenges. The use of big data and AI in policymaking raises concerns about privacy, surveillance, and the potential for biased or opaque decision-making processes. Moreover, the increasing reliance on digital platforms for government services can exacerbate the digital divide, leaving those without internet access or digital literacy at a disadvantage.

The future of governance will likely see a continued shift towards digital platforms and data-driven decision-making, but this must be balanced with strong protections for privacy, transparency, and inclusivity. Governments will need to ensure that the benefits of digital governance are accessible to all citizens, and that the risks associated with data use and technology are carefully managed.

Predictions from Experts and Visionaries About the Internet's Future

The Internet of Everything (IoE): Many experts predict that the future of the internet will involve the integration of the Internet of Things (IoT) into nearly every aspect of daily life, leading to the concept of the Internet of Everything (IoE). In this future, not only will devices and systems be connected, but so will people, processes, and data in a seamless digital ecosystem.

IoE envisions a world where smart cities, connected homes, autonomous vehicles, and wearable technology work together to create a highly efficient and personalized environment. For example, your smart home could anticipate your needs by adjusting lighting and temperature, your car could communicate with traffic systems to optimize your route, and your health could be monitored continuously by wearable devices that provide real-time feedback to healthcare providers.

While the IoE promises increased convenience, efficiency, and personalization, it also raises significant challenges related to privacy, security, and the ethical use of data. Ensuring that these technologies are developed and deployed in ways that respect individual rights and promote societal well-being will be critical to realizing the potential of the IoE.

The Metaverse: Another vision for the future of the internet is the development of the "metaverse," a collective virtual shared space created by the convergence of virtually enhanced physical reality and physically persistent virtual space, including virtual worlds, augmented reality (AR), and virtual reality (VR). The metaverse is seen as the next evolution of the internet, where users can interact with each other and digital environments in immersive, three-dimensional ways.

The concept of the metaverse has gained traction with the rise of platforms like Fortnite, Roblox, and VRChat, which allow users to create and explore virtual worlds, socialize, and engage in various activities. Tech giants like Facebook (now Meta) have also invested heavily in the development of the metaverse, envisioning it as the next major platform for social interaction, work, and entertainment.

In the metaverse, users could attend virtual events, collaborate on projects in digital workspaces, and even own and trade digital assets like virtual real estate and NFTs (non-fungible tokens). The metaverse could create new economic opportunities, cultural experiences, and ways of interacting that go beyond the limitations of the physical world.

However, the development of the metaverse also raises questions about digital ownership, identity, and the potential for digital inequality. As the metaverse becomes a more significant part of the internet, it will be important to ensure that it is accessible, inclusive, and governed by ethical standards that protect users' rights and foster positive social interactions.

The Decentralized Web (Web 3.0): Another key prediction for the future of the internet is the rise of the decentralized web, often referred to as Web 3.0. Unlike the current centralized model of the internet, where data and services are controlled by a few large companies, the decentralized web aims to distribute control and ownership across a network of users, using blockchain technology and decentralized protocols.

Web 3.0 envisions an internet where users have more control over their data and online identities, where digital transactions are secure and transparent, and where services are not dependent on centralized intermediaries. Decentralized applications (dApps) and decentralized finance (DeFi) are early examples of how this vision is taking shape, allowing users to interact directly with each other without relying on traditional financial institutions or tech companies.

The decentralized web has the potential to create a more open and equitable internet, reducing the power of monopolistic platforms and giving users greater autonomy. However, it also faces challenges related to scalability, usability, and regulatory oversight. As Web 3.0 technologies continue to develop, the balance between decentralization and regulation will be crucial in determining their impact on the future of the internet.

Expert Predictions and Visions: As we look to the future, experts and visionaries in technology, academia, and industry have offered a range of predictions about the internet's evolution. Some foresee the internet becoming even more deeply integrated into our daily lives, with advances in AI, IoT, and the metaverse creating new forms of interaction, work, and entertainment. Others warn of the potential risks, including increased surveillance, loss of privacy, and the concentration of power in the hands of a few large tech companies.

Tim Berners-Lee, the inventor of the World Wide Web, has advocated for a "new internet" that addresses the shortcomings of the current system, particularly issues related to data privacy and centralized control. His vision includes the development of technologies that allow users to own and control their data, as well as a more decentralized and open web that prioritizes user rights and freedom of expression.

Other experts emphasize the importance of ensuring that the internet remains a global, open, and inclusive platform. As geopolitical tensions and regulatory challenges increase, there is a risk that the internet could become fragmented, with different regions adopting their own rules and standards. Maintaining the global nature of the internet while addressing local needs and concerns will be a key challenge in the coming years.

Conclusion

The future of the internet is filled with both challenges and opportunities. Emerging technologies such as quantum computing, AI, the metaverse, and the decentralized web hold the potential to revolutionize how we interact, work, and live. At the same time, issues like net neutrality, open access, privacy, and security will continue to shape the internet's evolution and its impact on society.

As we navigate the complexities of the internet's future, it will be essential to balance innovation with ethical considerations, ensuring that the internet remains a force for good that promotes equality, freedom, and human well-being. The decisions we make today about the development and governance of the internet will have far-reaching consequences for generations to come.

The internet has come a long way from its humble beginnings, evolving into a global network that connects billions of people and drives the modern economy. As we look to the future, we must remain vigilant in addressing the challenges and seizing the opportunities that lie ahead, ensuring that the internet continues to be a platform for innovation, empowerment, and positive change.

www.ingramcontent.com/pod-product-compliance
Lightning Source LLC
Chambersburg PA
CBHW052152220526
45471CB00004B/1650